# DENMARK
# FINLAND
# ICELAND
# NORWAY
# SWEDEN

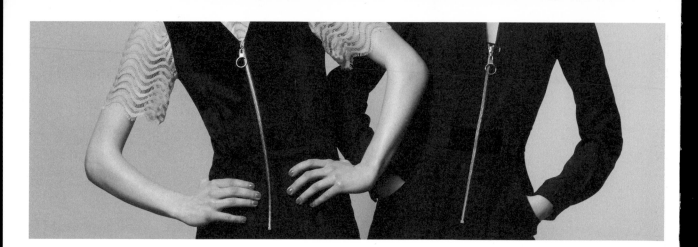

First published and distributed by
viction:workshop ltd.

# viction:ary™

viction:workshop ltd.
Unit C, 7/F, Seabright Plaza, 9-23 Shell Street,
North Point, Hong Kong
Url: www.victionary.com   Email: we@victionary.com

f @victionworkshop
🐦 @victionary_
📷 @victionworkshop

Edited and produced by viction:ary
Concepts & art direction by Victor Cheung
Book design by viction:workshop ltd.

Cover images courtesy of Normann Copenhagen, Heydays, Janine Rewell,
Lundgren+Lindqvist, BVD, and on the back, Siggeir Magnús Hafsteinsson.

ISBN 978-988-77747-0-9
Printed and bound in China

# TRULY
# NORDIC

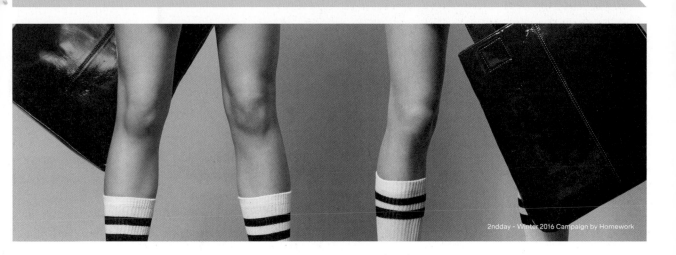

Less is more. More or less.

With a legacy in Scandinavian modernism and functionalism, contemporary Nordic design is routinely described as minimalist design characterised by simple forms, a restrained colour palette and strict typography. But to regard and define it merely by visual appearance only reveals a simplified understanding. If expressed in a single word, Nordic design should not be 'minimalist', but rather 'focused' as in marked by exactness and accuracy of expression. It is concerned with eliminating the superfluous and championing the essential, yet the reasoning is not for the sake of aesthetics, but for the sake of clarity and functionality. The distinctive visual expression should only be a consequence, not an objective in itself.

When at its most accomplished, Nordic design is so well-considered and so well balanced it might give the impression that it was created with little effort. It is however not easily attained, because when dealing with only the most essential, there is nothing to hide behind. Nothing can be judged quite so clearly like a design without embellishments. Every single aspect is in full focus, demanding careful attention to every last detail. Instead of an elaborate artistic expression, the achievement of Nordic design lies in the idea, the concept, and the tireless search for perfection.

Alongside other aspects of Scandinavian culture, like new Nordic cuisine and architecture, Nordic design is currently enjoying increased international attention. And looking forward, it might even be standing on the verge of a second coming. Carried forward by the digital evolution, the world of visual communication is becoming increasingly complex, with what seems to be an ever-evolving number of new media, channels

and platforms. In a world starved for attention and wildly focused on individuality, this speaks to the need for a more legible, straightforward and intelligent design language that is both scalable and will stand out from the chaos of bigger, louder, faster, more. These principles, along with the ideology of simple living, also fit well into the growing awareness of sustainability and resource-conscious consumption, influencing aesthetic values and promoting an appreciation of things that are basic, natural, and maybe even plain in appearance. In this context, the surest way forward is a clear and straightforward design approach, done with close attention to detail. It is very much possible to refine the elementary into the artful by pursuing consistency and clarity.

There is no question that the less-is-more motto captures the thinking behind Nordic design, but it is also a balance. Designers should never be dogmatic. We may be naturally influenced by our Scandinavian design heritage, but we should strive to maintain a global outlook and value the ability to both embrace and challenge diverse aesthetics.

Form follows function. The shape of a design should be based on its intended purpose. Understanding this principle really translates into endless stylistic possibilities. The only true rule is that the design should be suitable to the subject and in keeping with its functionality. That is why Nordic design should be regarded not as a stylistic convention, but as a guiding principle that sets the direction for an appropriate solution. Less is indeed more. But more can also be more.

**FEATURED
DESIGN UNITS**

**INTERVIEWS**

Stockholm Design Lab's lasting partnerships with IKEA and Scandinavian Airlines prove their knack for transforming brands remarkably unerring and persisting. Led by founder Björn Kusoffsky, the studio derives powerful solutions out of simple ideas, steeped in the Scandinavian tradition that stresses functionality, clarity and permanence. Kusoffsky's outstanding achievements in design were recognised by Berlingpriset in 2014 and Platinumegg in 2015.

# Stockholm
# Design Lab

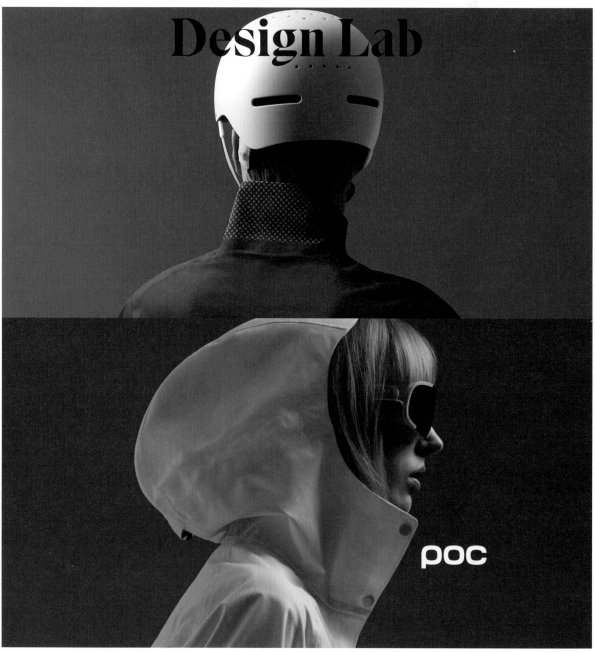

**01_ Poc and Forth, 2016.**
Images, brochure, hangtags, lookbook for Swedish
apparel brand Poc's first commuter collection.

STOCKHOLM DESIGN LAB ——008/009

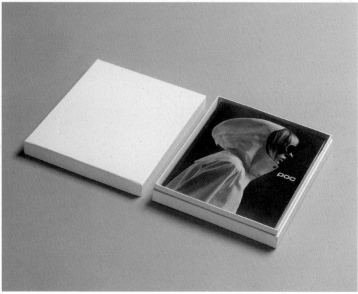

**02_Askul (Branding), 2005-15.**
Holistic visual identity for Japanese
office supplies brand Askul.

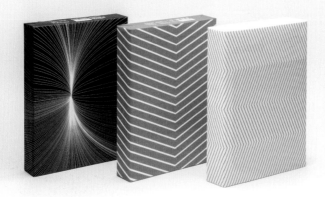

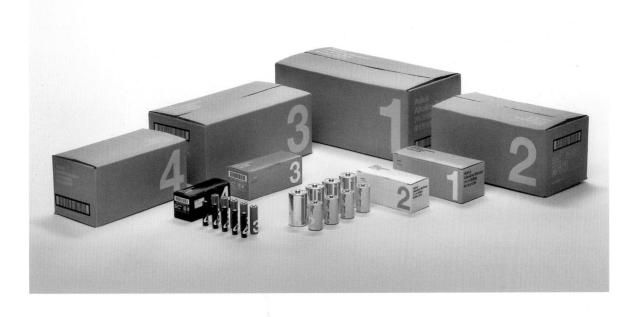

修正テープ
4.2mm×15m
10個入

4.2mm

#8

A6
Notebook
ノート・ブック

Askul
Ink Jet Paper
写真用
インクジェットペーパー
印画紙タイプ
Photo
Resin Coated Gloss
L Size

Askul
Glue Stick
スティックのり
40g

open here

おそうじ
汚れ用

Askul
Battery
アルカリ乾電池

1

2

3

4

Askul
Liquid Glue
Refill
補充液

400ml

**03_Askul Branded Products, 2005-15.**
Branded product designs for Askul's office
supply range, spanning from batteries,
medical bags and wet wipes.

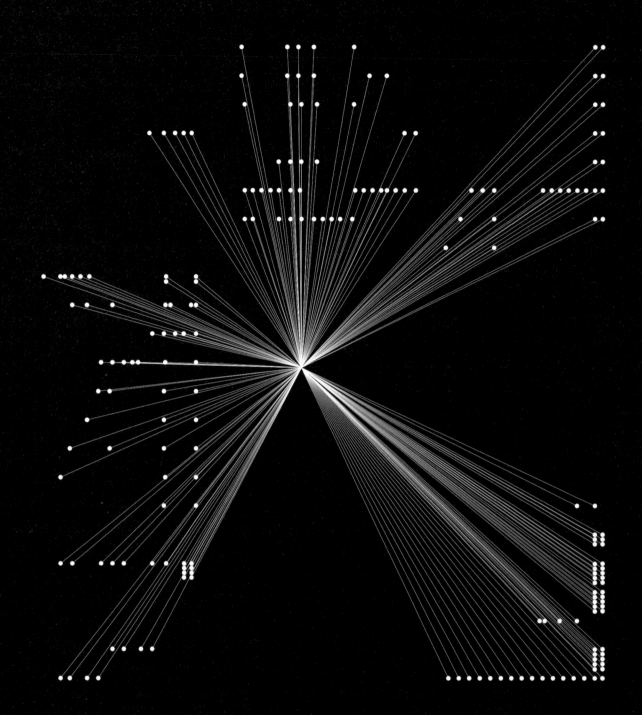

# "It's as much about functionality and context as the look and aesthetics."

–

STOCKHOLM DESIGN LAB

Full interview on page 183

**04_Ted Gärdestad, 2017.** Vinyl and CD covers, posters, and visuals for remastered album of the late Swedish singer Ted Gärdestad.

STOCKHOLM DESIGN LAB —— 014/015

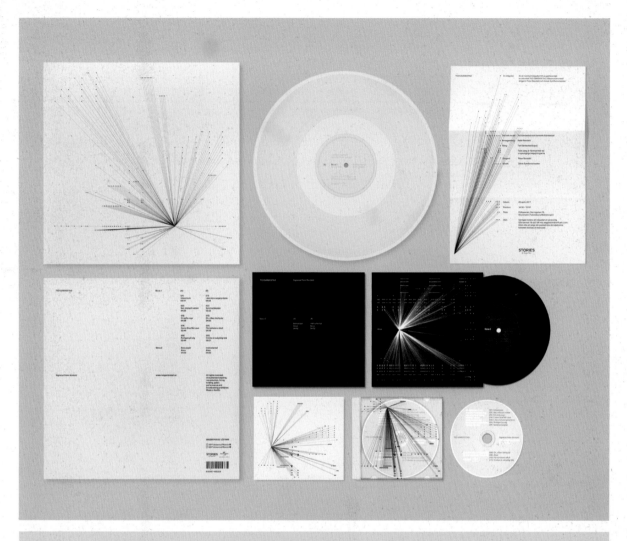

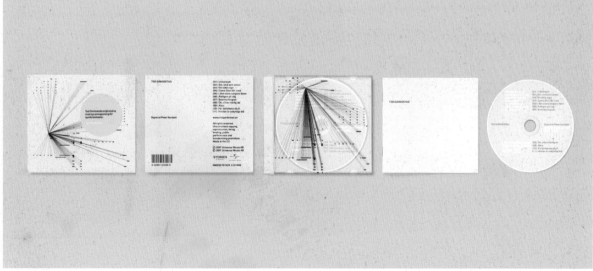

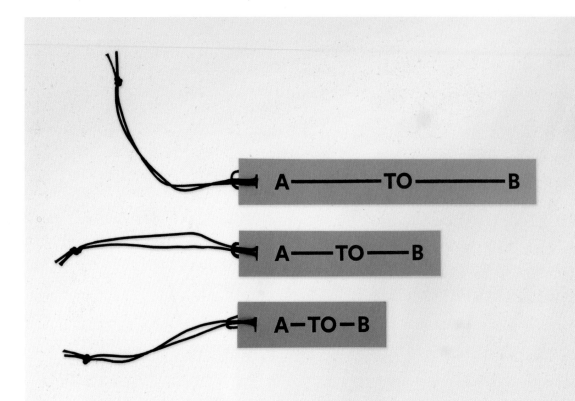

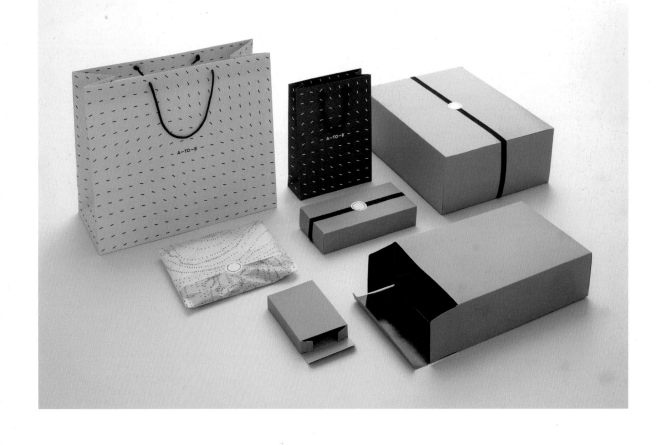

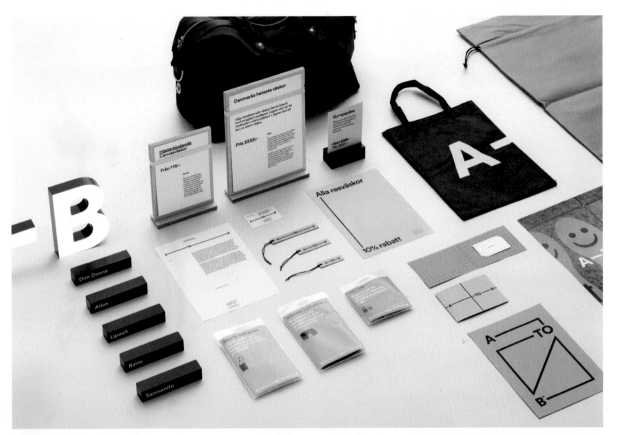

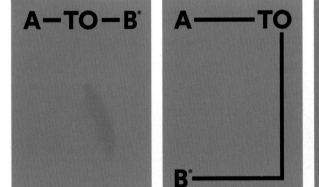

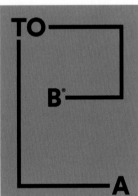

**05_A—TO—B, 2015.** Bag brand creation from concept to product design for Venue Retail Group.

BVD places simplicity above all others and provides clarity to brands, products and environments. A design and branding agency since 1996, they focus on strategic design projects for both small and large companies within wide-ranging fields. Their successful projects and simplifications work in a distinct four-step process: understanding brand functionality, finding the core of a brand, searching for an emotional driver, then maximising impact to audiences.

# BVD

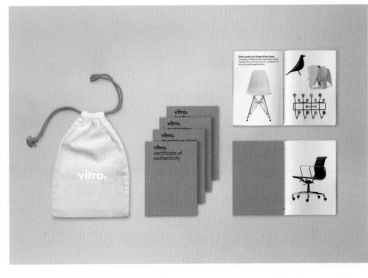

**01_Vitra Packaging Concept,
2014.** New concept to simplify and
uniform the packaging of the wide-
ranging Vitra products.

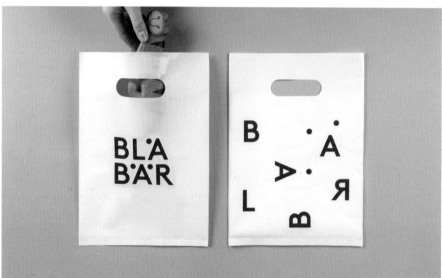

**02_Blå Bär, 2016.** Concept and visual identity for Scandinavian multi-brand shop Blå Bär's outlet in Osaka, Japan.

BVD —— 020/021

**03_Granit Body & Soul, 2017.**
Packaging for retail chain Granit's organic soap, lotion, and scented candle based on the idea of space.

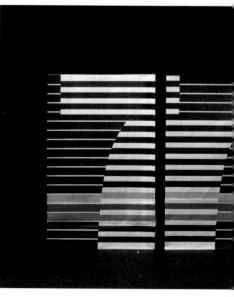

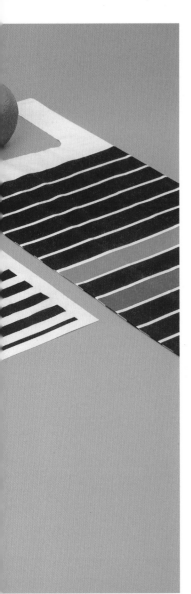

**04_7-Eleven Coffee Concept, 2014.** Brand update to refresh the coffee experience across 7-Eleven's outlets in Sweden.

BVD —— 024/025

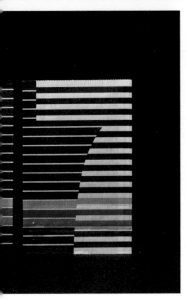

# Everyday elegance. Designed in Sweden.

# Made for you to use everyday.

**05_Bruk Brand Strategy & Design, 2016.**
Art direction to position glassworks
company Kosta Boda's new glassware
range as a young lifestyle collection.

**06_Bruk Visual Identity, 2016.**
Packaging and digital design for glassworks company Kosta Boda's new glassware range that speaks to young consumers.

Led by founding partners Andreas Friberg Lundgren and Carl-Johan Lindqvist, Lundgren+Lindqvist adopts the credo "design and development with purpose and precision". Conceptually driven, the team clarifies and renders brand stories across visual identities design, art direction, print, packaging, signage and digital applications, enabling a multi-layered brand experience. Lundgren+Lindqvist also runs publishing platform ll'Editions.

# Lundgren+Lindqvist

**01_Roger Burkhard Logo, 2017.** Monogram for a creative web development studio featuring a reversed capital 'R' for Roger, conjoined with a capital 'B' for Burkhard. Photo by Kalle Sanner.

**02_Roger Burkhard Stationery, 2017.** Promotional cards and responsive header underlie the creative web development studio's problem-solving attitude. Photos by Kalle Sanner.

LUNDGREN+LINDQVIST —— 028/029

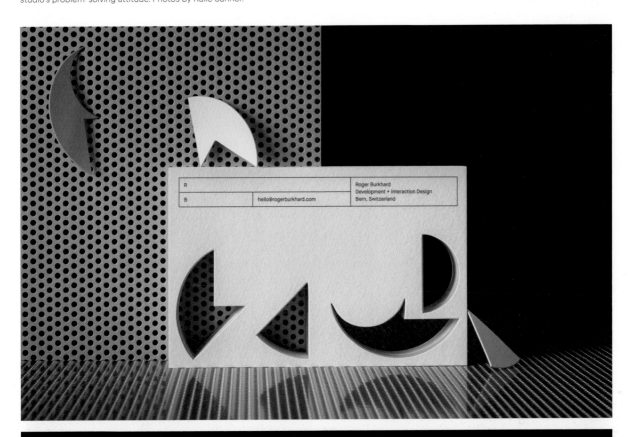

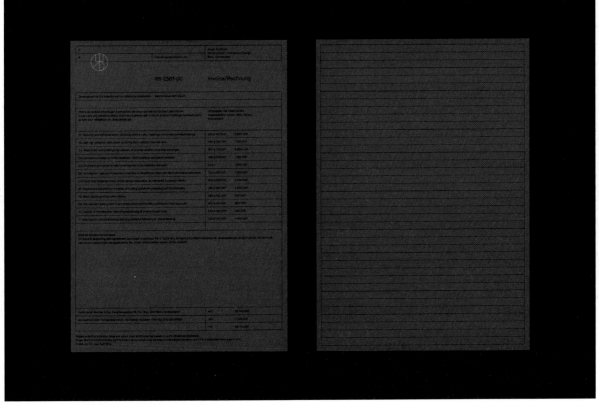

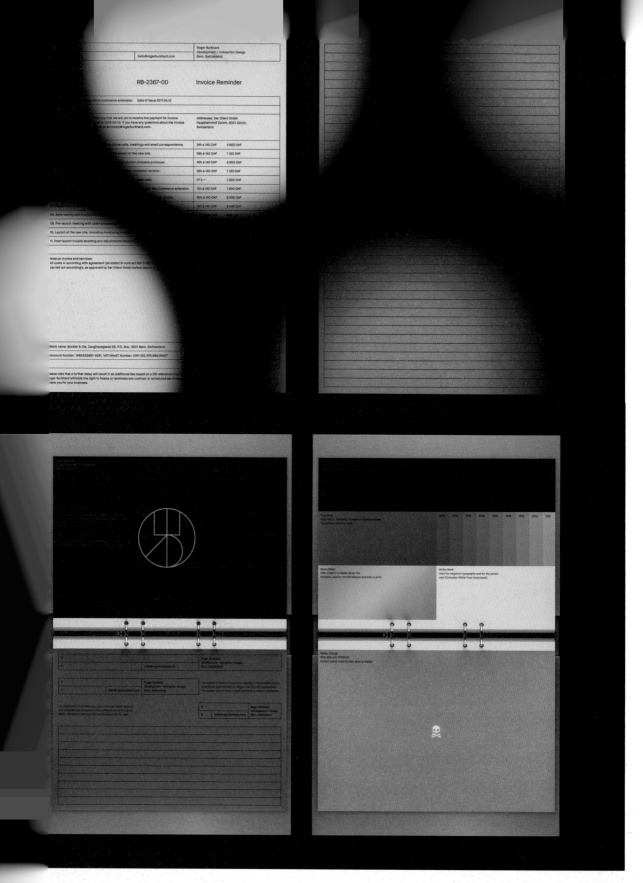

**Roger Burkhard Brand Identity, 2017.** Invoice reminder and brand guidelines for Swiss creative web elopment studio, Roger Burkhard. Photos by Kalle Sanner.

**04_100th Anniversary of the Contour Bottle, 2015.** Poster art for Coca-Cola, reimaging their vintage bottle imagery, inspired by Franz Kafka's *The Metamorphosis*.

MCKNGBRD

MCKNGBRD

[EMAIL] INFO@MCKNGBRD.COM [ONLINE] @MCKNGBRD.COM
[ADDRESS] 22800 LA PAZ ROAD, #003, ALISO VIEJO, CA 92656, UNITED STATES OF AMERICA

QUALITY AS A WAY OF LIFE

**05_MCKNGBRD, 2016.**
Visual identity for LA-based
laptop and tablet case
manufacturer MCKNGBRD.

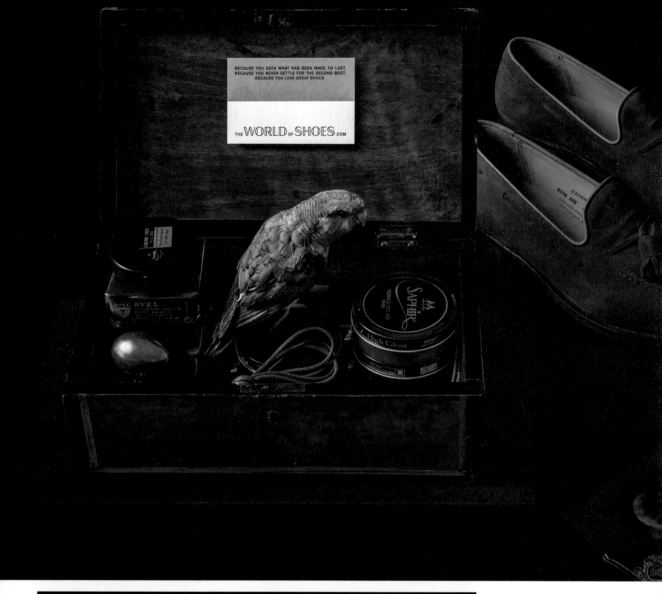

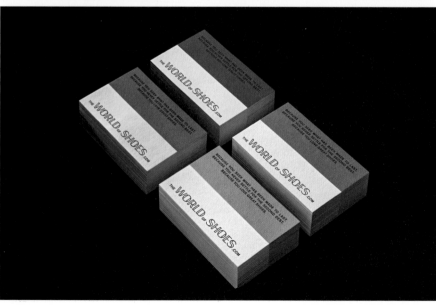

**06_The World of Shoes Brand Identity, 2016.** Business cards in different colourways convey a subtle eccentricity, referencing the quirky quality that pervades a dandy's outfit.

**07_The World of Shoes Web Design, 2016.**
Web design for an online platform focussing on men's
handmade shoes. Photos by Kalle Sanner.

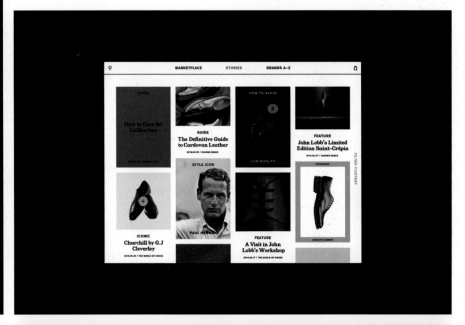

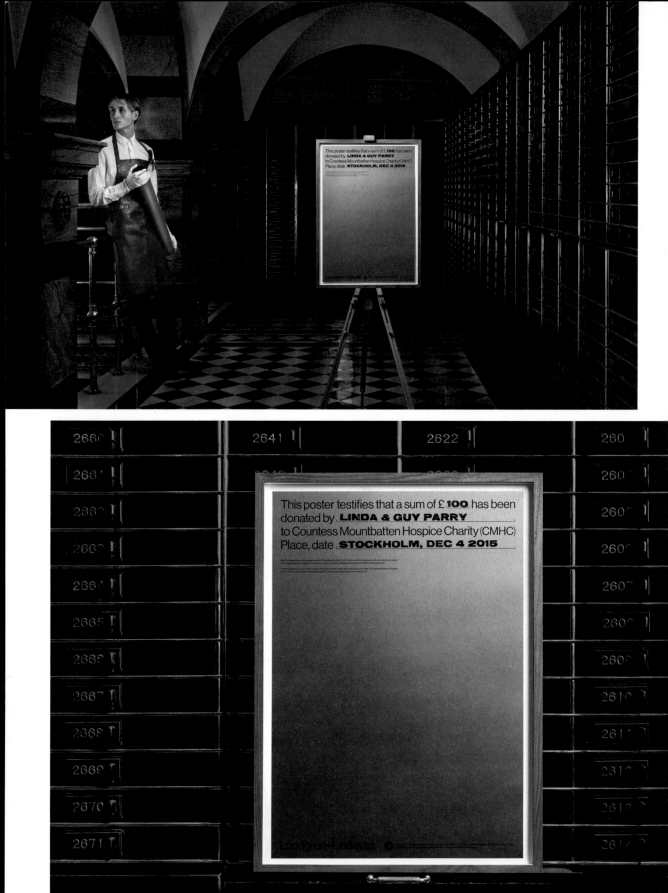

This poster testifies that a sum of £ **100** has been donated by **LINDA & GUY PARRY** to Countess Mountbatten Hospice Charity (CMHC) Place, date **STOCKHOLM, DEC 4 2015**

**08_Nifty-50, 2015.** Poster art created on the theme of "money" auctioned to raise funds for Countess Mountbatten Hospice Charity. Photos by Kalle Sanner.

**09_Ord/Bild Notebooks, 2016.** Special edition notebook set with a numbered token held by a staple-bound box. Photos by Kalle Sanner.

Working between Copenhagen and Tokyo, design agency Kontrapunkt advocates the value of being genuine. Their designs seek the essence of a brand, translating human needs and winning ideas into meaningful brand experiences, uniting form and function in true Scandinavian fashion. Enriching and animating, Kontrapunkt engages with a strong ecosystem of specialised partners, with more than 60 specialists in their offices.

**Copenhagen, Denmark**
**Tokyo, Japan**

• branding • identity • typography

# Kontrapunkt

**01_Danish Design Award Identity, 2016.**
Visual identity, brand typeface and venue
graphics for the annual Danish Design Award.

DANISH DESIGN AWARD **CELEBRATES** THE **DIFFERENCE** DESIGN MAKES — EVEN **BEYOND** OUR **IMAGINATION.** THE **AWARD** COVERS 11 CATEGORIES FROM **BUSINESS** DESIGN AND **SERVICE** DESIGN TO **EXPERIENCE** DESIGN, **BROADENING** OUR **CONCEPT OF DESIGN** AND HOW DESIGN MAKES OUR **LIVES BETTER,** HEALTHIER AND HAPPIER. DANISH DESIGN AWARD WANTED A **VISUAL IDENTITY** THAT MATCHED THE **HIGH QUALITY** OF THE PROJECTS **NOMINATED.** AND MORE IMPORTANTLY, A VISUAL IDENTITY THAT **SUPPORTS** THE OVER-ALL MESSAGE: **DESIGN MAKES A DIFFER-ENCE.** WE STARTED BY **LOOKING BACK.** DANISH DESIGN HAS A LONG, PROUD TRADITION FOR **HUMANISTIC** AND **DEMOCRATIC** DESIGN. ESPECIALLY THE **EARLY MODERNIST** AND DAN-ISH DESIGN **PIONEER KNUD V. ENGELHARDT'S** TYPOGRAPHIC WORK BECAME **KEY** IN OUR SEARCH FOR **INSPIRATION.** SO WE DECIDED TO DESIGN A **NEW TYPOGRAPHY** THAT WE CALLED **"DANISH",** BASED ON ENGEL-HARDT'S **FUNCTIONALISTIC AESTHETICS.** THEN WE LOOKED **FORWARD.** WE WORKED WITH **TIGHT** AND **"CHUNKY"** TYPEFACE COMPOSI-TIONS AND **BLACK** AND **WHITE** GRAPHICS TO GIVE IT A **CONTEMPORARY** TOUCH AND NOT GET TOO **NOSTALGIC.** THE RESULT IS A VISUAL IDENTITY THAT **CAPTURES** THE **COMBINATION** OF **TRADITION** AND **INNOVATION** IN A **RECOG-NIZABLE** FONT. **TOGETHER** WITH THE **TIGHT** AND **SIMPLE** GRAPHICAL UNIVERSE THE TYPE-FACE GIVES DANISH DESIGN AWARD A **STRONG VOICE** TO PROMOTE THE **POWER OF DESIGN.**

DANISH DESIGN AWARD

SHA
RE RE
SOU
RCES

D

HE
A
LTH
Y LI
FE

D

WE CEL
EBRATE
THE DIFF
ERENCE
DESIGN
CAN
MAKE

D

**02_Danish Design Award Promotional
Campaign, 2016.** Type-based posters and
promotional materials for the annual Danish
Design Award.

abcdefghijklmnopqrstuvwxyzæøå
ABCDEFGHIJKLMNOPQRSTUVWXYZÆØÅ
12345678901234567890

abcdefghijklmnopqrstuvwxyzæøå
ABCDEFGHIJKLMNOPQRSTUVWXYZÆØÅ
12345678901234567890

abcdefghijklmnopqrstuvwxyzæøå
ABCDEFGHIJKLMNOPQRSTUVWXYZÆØÅ
12345678901234567890

abcdefghijklmnopqrstuvwxyzæøå
ABCDEFGHIJKLMNOPQRSTUVWXYZÆØÅ
12345678901234567890

←↖↑↗→↘↓↙  ←↖↑↗→↘↓↙

23
Spor Track

**04_DSB Brand System, 1994-.**
Brand typeface and signage design
for Danish State Railways.

**05_ASICS Tiger Typeface, 2016.**
Brand typeface design as part of the sports lifestyle brand's relaunch campaign, created in hands with Bruce Mau Design. Photos by Bruce Mau Design.

ASICSTIGER BRAND TYPEFACE

# VOL.1

ABCDEFGHIJKLMNOPQRSTUVWXYZACEFJKMNORWXY
0123456789012345678£€¥$#0&PIⅢⅤ*+

# THE REBIRTH OF AN ICON

**06_The Carlsberg Foundation Brand Typeface, 2015.** Bespoke typeface and logo recreated based on the curves of the hop plant and the original logo introduced in 1904.

**07_Carlsberg Beer Can, 2015.**
Packaging for Carlsberg Germany taking the hop leaf as a principal element in the temporary design.

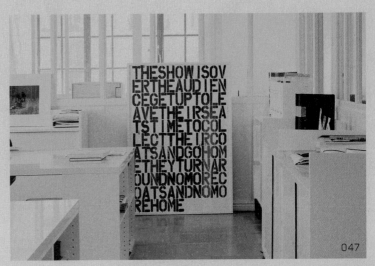

STOCKHOLM
/SWEDEN

## What define(s) good design?

Good design expresses ideas in a simplified and clear way. To achieve this, BVD approaches each job with the philosophy of "Simplify to Clarify".

## What was your vision when you started your practice?

We observed so many things that we thought could be designed and communicated in a much easier and cleverer way. As often as not, packaging and logo designs were too complicated and too messy that they failed to do the job.

## How would you describe your creative style?

We try to reduce all clutter, find the core and from there evoke emotions to get maximum impact. Our design is clear, simple, strong and honest.

That's our central philosophy and we call it "Simplify to Clarify". Working with it is both challenging and inspiring. Every day, our lives are fragmented with all these messages and decisions. It's easy to feel stressed from constant time constraints in our busy lives. We long for more simplicity and harmony. We need space and interspace to see things in this noisy environment. In a shopping centre, for example, it's easy to be overwhelmed by impressions.

048

**The Design S Award, 2014**
Prize design for the 2014 edition, crafted using Swedish paper.

When a client wants to make a packaging stand out, we need to find the empty space, or make space — so that the essential message becomes visible. The easiest way to achieve simplicity is through thoughtful reduction and sustainability. Cut the crap and let the core message reach the consumer.

**What draw(s) you to stay in Sweden to work?**

From a professional point of view the geographical placement of the studio is less important nowadays. All of us were born in Sweden, so the Scandinavian design language is in our blood, like a cultural tradition. We have lots of space and access to nature here. We believe in a sustainable world and circular economy, and are proud that Sweden is one of the leading countries in these two areas.

**What are your biggest influences? How do they work their way into your creations?**

The Nordic landscape has a huge impact on us and it shows in our simple and clean design. Most of the year our landscape is coloured in a dull, subtle blue, white, grey, brownish palette. It's calm, quiet, and harmonious. Some people think it's cold, but we love it. We find it very inspiring to jump back and forth between the modern busy Stockholm city life to the quiet and calm nature.

**Can you name one thing that people normally would mistake and one thing people should know about the "Nordic style"?**

We do not know exactly what the "Nordic Style" is, but for sure many things designed in the Scandinavian countries are connected with words like beauty, function and simplicity. For us simplicity is where aesthetics, beauty and function originate from. We solve problems with design and make it work. Everyone wants something that is effective, functional and able to talk to your feelings.

**Any upcoming projects?**

We don't want to jinx anything by talking about it. Keep an eye on bvd.se. New projects continuously pop up there.

## TEAM

**Carin Blidholm Svensson,
Catrin Vagnemark**
Founders & Creative Directors

**Diana Uppman**
CEO

**Karin Bergerham**
COO

**Rikard Ahlberg**
Design Director

**Kicki Ekberg**
Senior Strategic Advisor

**Minna Salo, Sofia Langheim**
Project Managers

**Kina Giesenfeld**
Art Director

**Tom Eriksson**
Senior Designer & Digital Creative

**Bengt Anderung,
Freja Hedvall,
Victor Kanmert**
Graphic Designers

**Fredrik Axelsson**
Industrial Designer

Neumeister's brand designs scream out-of-the-ordinary approaches but "think outside the box" is not entirely their creative drive. Driven by a business mind and a designer's eye, the brand agency has been visualising visions and refreshing brands since 2006. In 2013, they added an office in Malmö, and continue to manifest their belief in "revision, evolution, revolution" in brand design.

Stockholm, Sweden
Malmö, Sweden

• branding • art direction
• editorial

# Neumeister
# Strategic Design

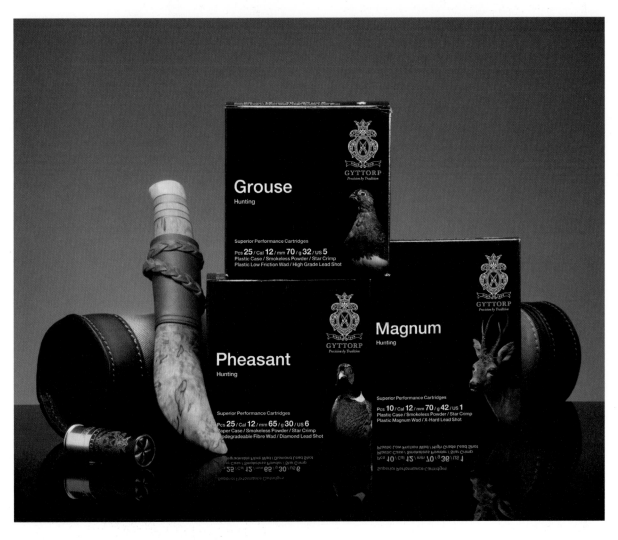

**01_Gyttorp Rebranding, 2011.** Visual identity and packaging to breathe new life into one of Sweden's long established hunting equipment suppliers' brand.

02_Gyttorp Packaging, 2011.
Ideas of precision and tradition
inform Gyttorp's new packaging.

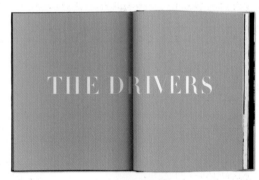

**03_Two Days in Monte Carlo, 2012.**
Book design for *Two Days in Monte Carlo*, profiling photographer Sture Lindvall's documentation of the 25th Monaco Grand Prix in 1967.

Graphic identity for restaurant
Nosh and Chow which serves
a medley of gastronomic
experiences in Stockholm.

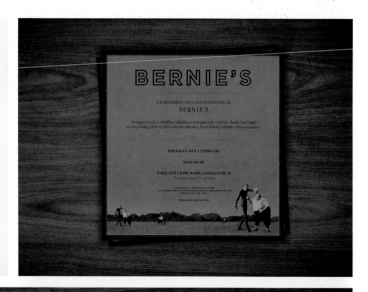

**05_LoLa, 2016.** Packaging design for craft beer LoLa, a collaboration between South American restaurant Supper and Brutal Brewing in Stockholm.

Founded by creative director Jack Dahl, Homework is both a graphic design studio and creative consultancy that specialises in brand expression, visual identity, art direction and more. They have collaborated with and developed long term relationships with respected international brands in fashion, lifestyle, beauty and luxury, providing them with aspirational and creative strategies that boost a contemporary aesthetic.

# Homework

**01_Organic Aroma Packaging, 2015.**
Packaging design for chef Kille Enna's
premium botanical extracts.

**02_2ndday Brand Identity, 2017.** Visual identity and packaging for a
Danish-Scandinavian woman's label stressing quality and slick tailoring.
Photo by Niklas Højlund.

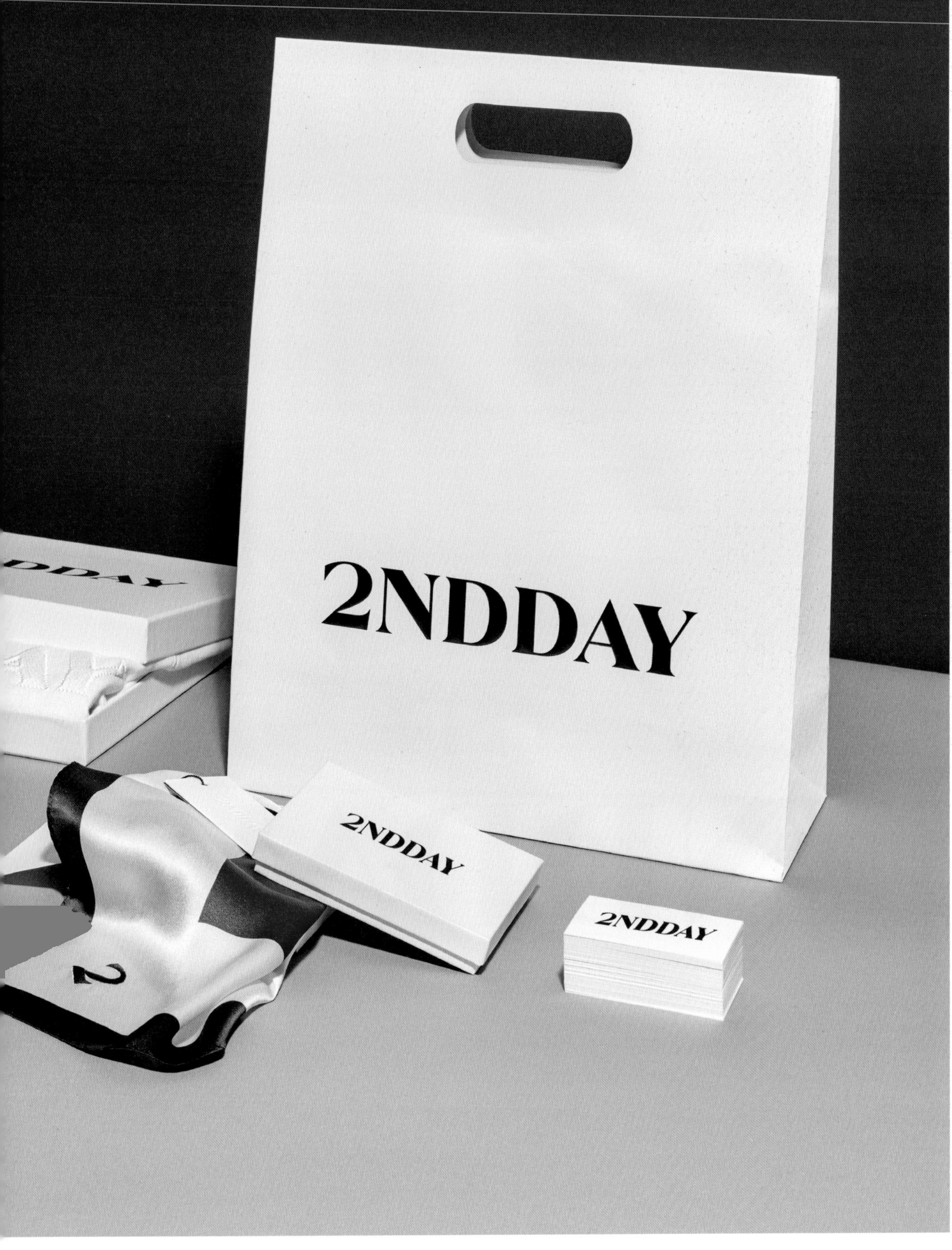
2NDDAY
2NDDAY
2NDDAY

# 2NDDAY

**03_2ndday — Winter 2016 Campaign, 2016.**
Campaign art direction for women's fashion atelier
2ndday. Photos by Elisabeth Toll. Creative direction
by Blank Atelier. Styling by Robert Rydberg. Hair
by Karolina Liedberg, Makeup by Josefina Zarmen.
Models from Nish Management.

**04_2ndday — Winter 2015 Campaign, 2015.** Campaign art direction for 2ndday. Photos by Magnus Magnusson. Creative direction by Blank Atelier. Styling by Robert Rydberg. Hair & Makeup by Rikke Dengsø. Models from Nish Management.

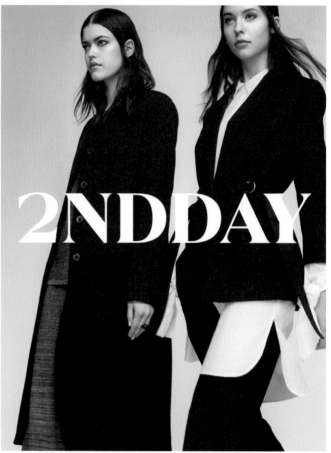

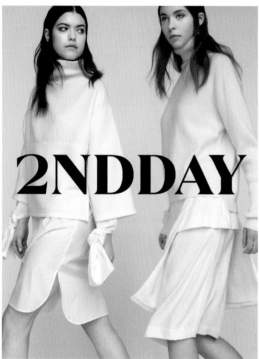

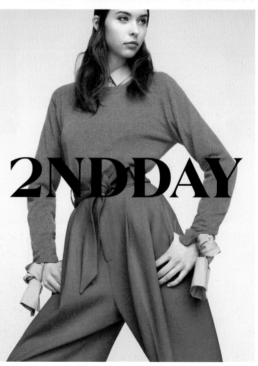

# "We challenge the way people feel and think by making design matter."

–

Homework

Full interview on page 283

**05_Intermission DK, 2013.** Editorial design, graphic design, and art direction for Intermission magazine. Photos by John Scarisbrick.

**06_Addition Adelaide — Press Invitations, 2015-16.** Multi-layered press invites for Addition Adelaide Tokyo's Spring/Summer 2016 (above) and Autumn/Winter 2015 (left) show.

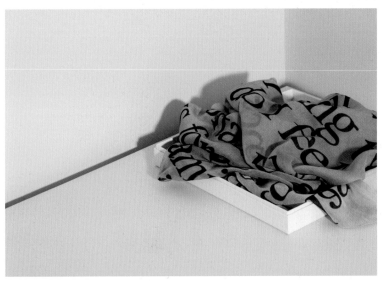

**07_Masai — Typographic Manifesto, 2016.** Visual identity and graphic design for fashion and lifestyle brand Masai.

**08_Studio David Thulstrup, 2016.** Visual identity and print collateral developed in collaboration with the architecture, interior and design practice based in Copenhagen.

Danish designer Claus Due and Swedish-born Tor Weibull demonstrate their typographic prowess and strong eyes for conceptual storytelling under the name Studio Claus Due. Working in the field of art and culture, the graphic design duo creates unique voices in both digital and print means. While Claus Due previously practised as Designbolaget, winning recognitions from international awards, Tor Weibull is most noted for his experimental type designs.

# Studio Claus Due

FRIENDS WITH BOOKS

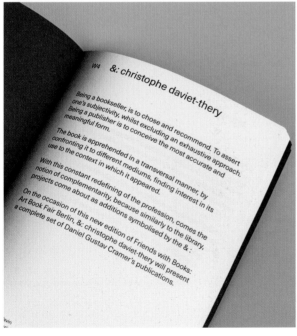

**01_Friends with Books, 2015-.**
Visual identity for Art Book Fair
Berlin, which promotes international
contemporary art book publishing.

**02_FÆNGSLET Visual Identity, 2014.** Website, signage, stationery, merchandise and communications design for a museum and cultural venue FÆNGSLET, inhabiting the former Horsens State Prison.

**03_Man and God, 2016.** Publication designed as an 'animated' response to the exhibition "Man and God" in Boston, questioning the relationship between God and man.

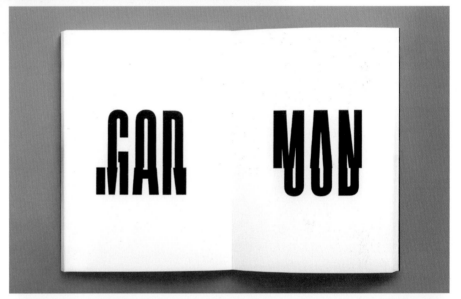

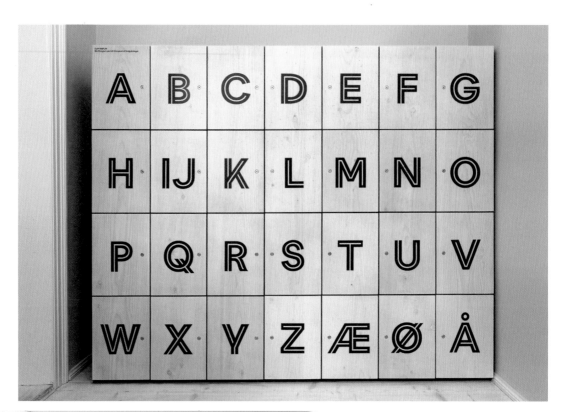

**04_CLAY Visual Identity, 2015.**
Name, logo, custom typeface, printed materials, signage and website design for the Museum of Ceramic Art Denmark.

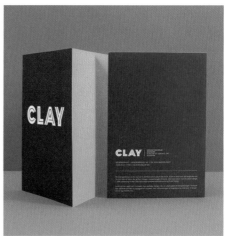

**05_The Danish Shipowners'
Association, 2013-16.** Visual
identity for the Danish Shipowners'
Association and its annuals.

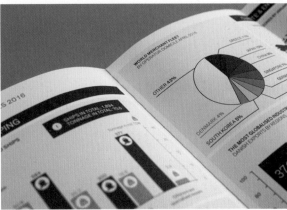

**06_X-Room Visual Identity, 2013.**
Visual system based around the
letter 'X' for the programmes of
X-Room, the experimental art
space inside the National Gallery of
Denmark.

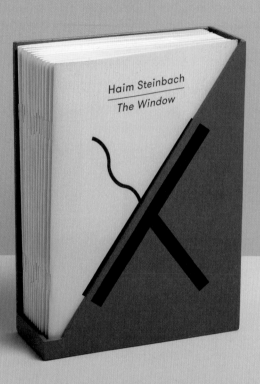

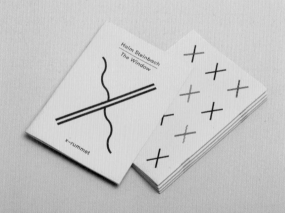

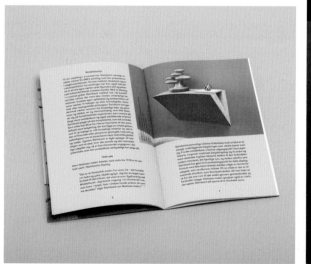

**07_X-Room Visual Identity, 2013.**
Logo modifications represent a different artist featured at the National Gallery of Denmark's experimental space, X-Room.

**08_ecal workshop, 2016.** Propaganda posters created by ECAL students during a three-day workshop run by Studio Claus Due.

Every company has a great story to tell, and Heydays aims to tell them through focused and functional identities that stand out in both commercial and cultural areas. Established in 2008, by Mathias Haddal Hovet, Lars Kjelsnes, Martin Sanne Kristiansen, Thomas Lein and Stein Henrik Haugen, the studio is dedicated to bringing progressive brands to life in both print and digital means. Throughout the years, they have built a solid client base, comprised of start-ups and established names.

# Heydays

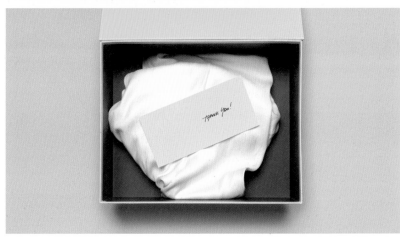

**01_Gaggu Vintage, 2015.** Visual identity, packaging and web design for a vintage bridal salon which offers a unique range of wedding gowns from the 1920s up to the 1990s.

"From ambitious start-ups to deep-rooted companies with generations of history, every company has a great story to tell. We bring progressive brands to life through focused and functional identities, so products and story can be understood."

–

HEYDAYS

Full interview at page 223

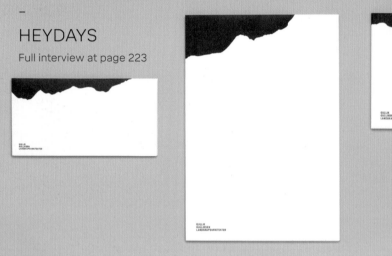

**02_Gullik Gulliksen
Landskapsarkitekter, 2016.**
Visual identity and web design for
Norwegian landscape architectural
firm, Gullik Gulliksen.

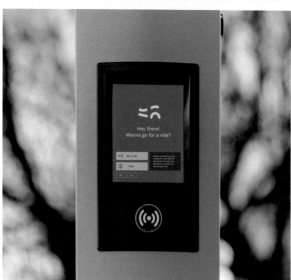

**03_Oslo City Bike, 2016.** Brand
strategy, visual identity, UI design,
and motion graphics for Oslo's city
bike system.

**04_Wesley Mann, 2015.** Visual identity and stationery design for American portrait photographer Wesley Mann.

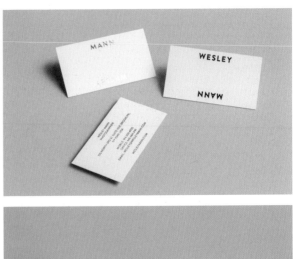

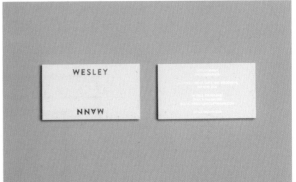

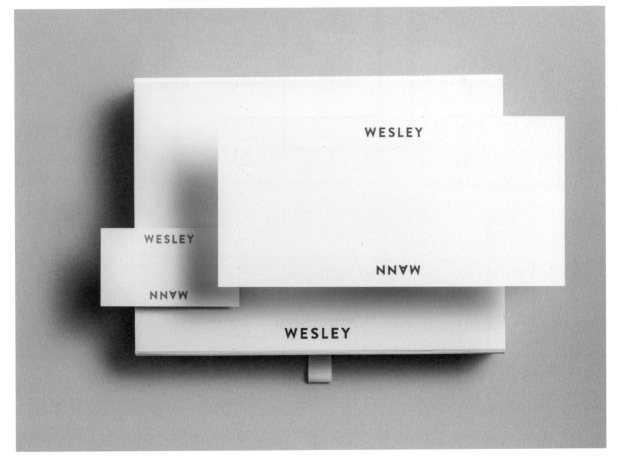

Established in 1999, strategic design agency Re-public specialises in branding and visual identity, developing intelligent and innovative cross-platform design solutions. Award-winning and highly collaborative, their craftsmanship is highly valued from Copenhagen to Mexico City. Thriving on long-term and honest partnerships, Re-public builds meaningful and detailed visual communication that embraces diversity in both their clientele and aesthetics.

# Re-public

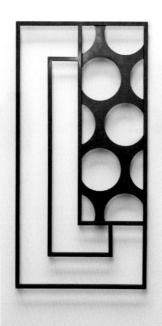

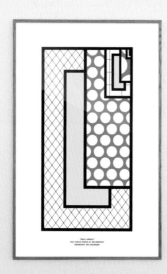

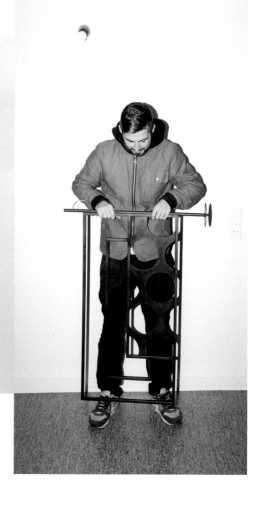

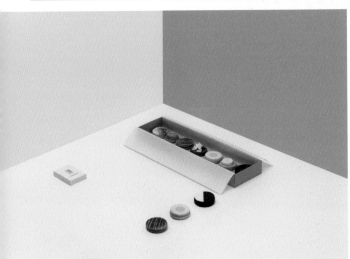

**01_Leckerbaer Visual identity, 2015.** Packaging, stationery, and shop front design for pastry shop Leckerbaer which takes pride in reinterpreting Danish classics. Photo by Maria Schumann.

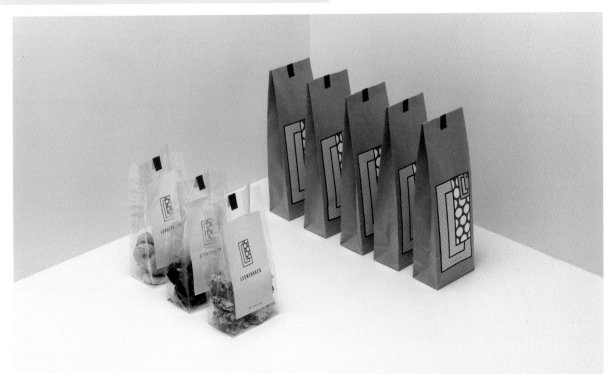

"If expressed in a single word, Nordic design should not be 'minimalist', but rather 'focused', as in marked by exactness and accuracy of expression."

—

RE-PUBLIC

**02_Leckerbaer Posters, 2015.** Art direction
and photography to highlight the pastry shop's
craftsmanship and the qualities in Leckerbaer's
stand-out products. Photo by Line Falck.

**03_Gold—Smidt Assembly Visual Identity, 2016.** Logo, stationery, mobile logo-lightbox, brand concept, and digital design for new art gallery Gold—Smidt Assembly, with focus on presenting "the art of curating". Photos by Romeo Vidner.

Facing page-bottom: Counterpoint
in the Chapel. Reproduced with the
permission of Chartworth House Trust.

# NORD

**NORD**

**CENTRO**

B

DOCUMENTO QUE
EVIDENCIE LA TRAYECTORIA
Y EXPERIENCIA DE LOS
EMPRENDEDORES:
PREMIOS,
RECONOCIMIENTOS,
LOGROS, ACTIVIDADES
PREVIAS, FORMACIÓN,
ASOCIACIONES,
ENTRE OTROS.

# CENTR

**04_Nord Centro Visual Identity, 2015.**
Poster, stationery, and web design,
creating a fusion of styles for Mexican
furniture brand Nord Centro.

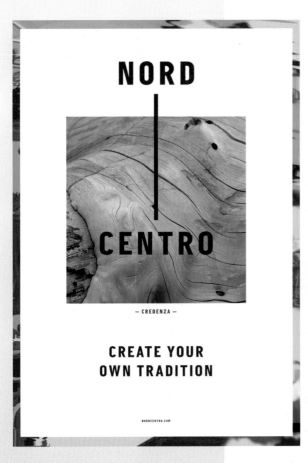

**NORD | CENTRO**

— CREDENZA —

**CREATE YOUR OWN TRADITION**

NORDCENTRO.COM

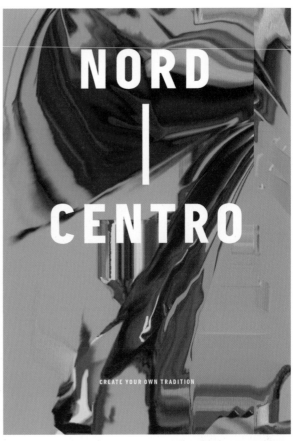

**NORD | CENTRO**

CREATE YOUR OWN TRADITION

**05_Nord Centro Brand Development, 2016.** Visual identity,
stationery, posters, and web design demonstrate the kind of clear
direction NCBD can offer as a management consultancy. Photos
by Line Falck.

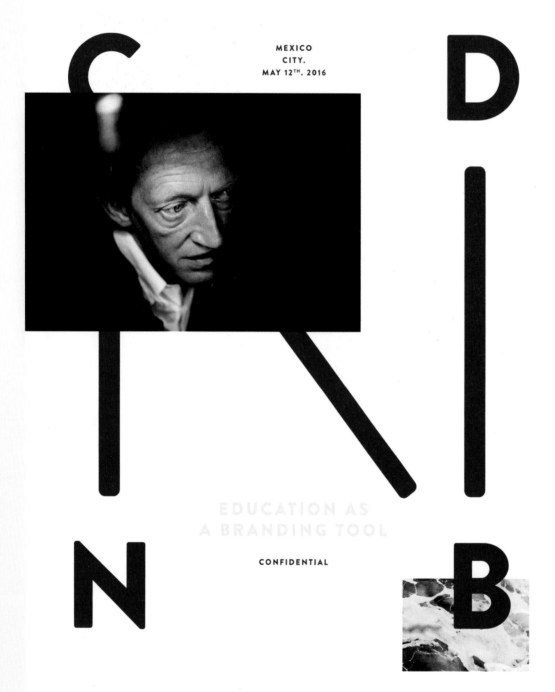

MEXICO
CITY.
MAY 12TH. 2016

EDUCATION AS
A BRANDING TOOL

CONFIDENTIAL

NORD CENTRO
BRAND DEVELOPMENT

*This report is solely for the use of client personnel. No part of it may be circulated, quoted, or reproduced for
distribution outside the client organization. This material was used by Nord Centro Brand Development during an oral presentation;
it is not a complete record of the discussion.*

**06_Permanent Daylight, 2013.** Publication combining
the formats of book, newspaper and magazine to hold
selected works by Jonas Liveröd with notes, interviews
and more. Photos by Jenny Nordquist.

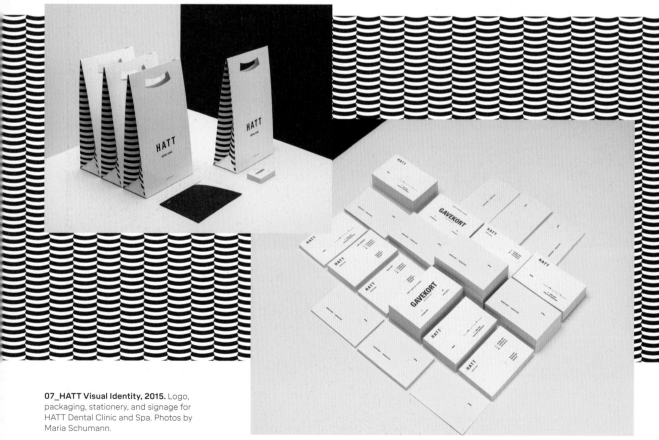

**07_HATT Visual Identity, 2015.** Logo, packaging, stationery, and signage for HATT Dental Clinic and Spa. Photos by Maria Schumann.

OSLO
/NORWAY
VIENNA
/AUSTRIA

**What define(s) good design?**

Design should be engaging, useful, functional, and question the status quo.

**What was your vision when you started your practice?**

When we started Bleed in 2000 just when the internet bubble bursted. We all came from companies that had grown from five to infinity in a very short time. The culture was superficial and success was defined by growth and not quality. We wanted to run a studio that created work we care about. We wanted to build a smaller but focused team who wanted to make change happen.

**How would you describe your creative style?**

As a studio we don't want to be stuck with one style aesthetically. What we share is more an approach that challenges the segments we work within. We use a lot of time in the concept phase prototyping ideas.

**What draw(s) you to stay in Norway to work?**

Nature, fresh air, and authentic people.

**What are your biggest influences? How do they work their way into your creations?**

I think the clarity and the "no bullshit" way of Norwegian culture is important to our work. Norwegians are not overly polite, no unnecessary pleasantries. We talk directly and this is also very much how we approach work.

**How do you ensure ideas/messages can be communicated effectively through your work?**

We spend a lot of time to get to know our clients, the projects and their goals. Before drawing a line we work our methods finding the perfect concept. Fine tuning this part of design makes the result meaningful and interesting.

**Can you name one thing that people normally would mistake and one thing people should know about the "Nordic style"?**

I think some think it just means being "simple". The truth is that it is functional and to the point.

**Any upcoming projects?**

Many interesting projects but I can't talk about for now! Keep an eye out on our website and watch this space!

### TEAM

**Svein Haakon Lia**
**Dag Laska**
Creative Directors & Founding Partners

**Kjell Reenskaug**
Creative Director & Partner

**Astrid Feldner**
Design Director & Associate (Vienna)

**Marie Louise Notøy Steen,**
**Alette Schei Rørvik**
Project Managers

**Kristoffer Lundberg**
Senior Designer & Developer

**Camille Dorival,**
**Bjørnar Pedersen,**
**Listya Amelia,**
**Madeleine Eriksen,**
**Marc Damm,**
**Nicolas Vittori,**
**William Stormdal**
Designers

**Pedro Pereira**
Designer & Developer

Established in 1997 with a mission to nurture and release the powerful force of good ideas, branding agency Happy F&B has a firm belief in a collectivist approach. Far-sighted strategy and smart design evolve side by side in their design, resulting in smart solutions that can endure changes with great impact. Happy F&B is part of the Forsman & Bodenfors group and MDC Partners, which also run their own ad agencies and production houses.

Gothenburg, Sweden
Stockholm, Sweden

• branding • identity
• packaging

# Happy F&B

**01_The Söderberg Prize: Henrik Vibskov, 2011.** Catalogue design celebrates the fashion designer as 2011's prize winner, with forms taken from his conceptual world.

"Besides the characteristic balloon, the sequence forms a link to one of Bronger's most fundamental theme - time."

–

HAPPY F&B

**02_The Söderberg Prize: Sigurd Bronger, 2012.** Catalogue design inspired by the individuality and humour in the 2012 winner's work.

**03_The Söderberg Prize: Hjalti Karlsson, 2013.** Catalogue design highlighting the existence of the 2013 winner's work partner, who could not share the Nordic award for his German nationality.

**04_The Söderberg Prize: Ilkka Suppanen, 2015.** Catalogue design illustrating the winner's philosophy: if we are to survive on this planet, then what goes around must also come around.

Röhsska museets katalog nr. 23 för
Torsten och Wanja Söderbergs pris 2016
Margrethe Odgaard, Danmark

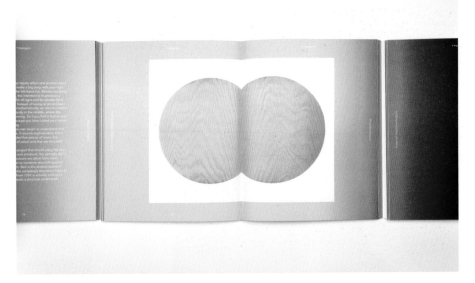

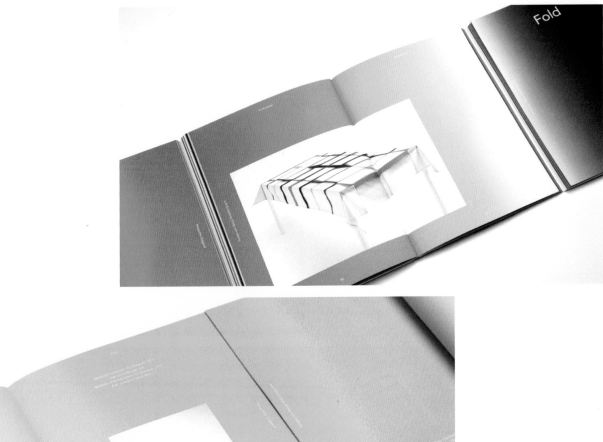

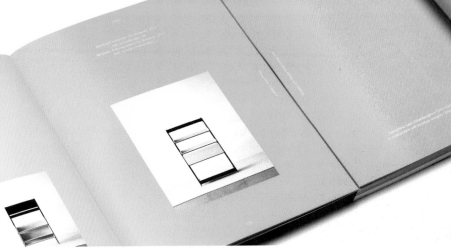

**05_The Söderberg Prize:
Margrethe Odgaard, 2016.**
Catalogue design celebrating the
winner's favourite shades, nuances,
and passion that charges her work.

**06_GöteborgsOperan, 2017.** Visual identity and typeface design for the Swedish Opera House that regularly stages operas and musicals as well as classical and contemporary ballet.

**07_Orio, 2013.** Brand strategy and visual identity for automobile spare parts supplier Orio, previously known as Saab Parts.

HAPPY F&B ⸺ 110/111

Henrik Nygren sees graphic design as an important form of communication. Where clearness and direction reinforce clarity, the designer stresses on the sensual touch of prints. Pursuing beauty in functionality and precision like an architect, Nygren has undoubtedly left his mark with his modernist designs for books, exhibitions, and brand communications, done closely with his network of specialists and his clients. The 2014 book, *Grafisk design: Henrik Nygren*, catalogues his achievements between 1991—2013.

# Henrik Nygren Design

**01_I—X Identity, 2016.** Visual identity for Form Us With Love's retrospective exhibition, as an extension of their new corporate identity, to mark their first decade as a design studio.

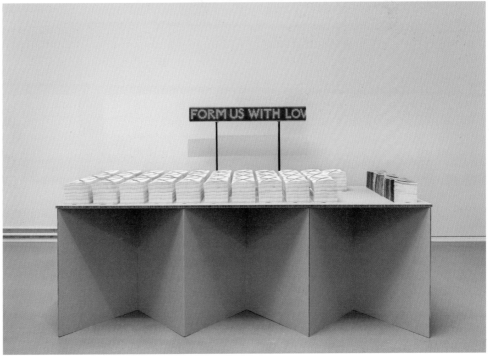

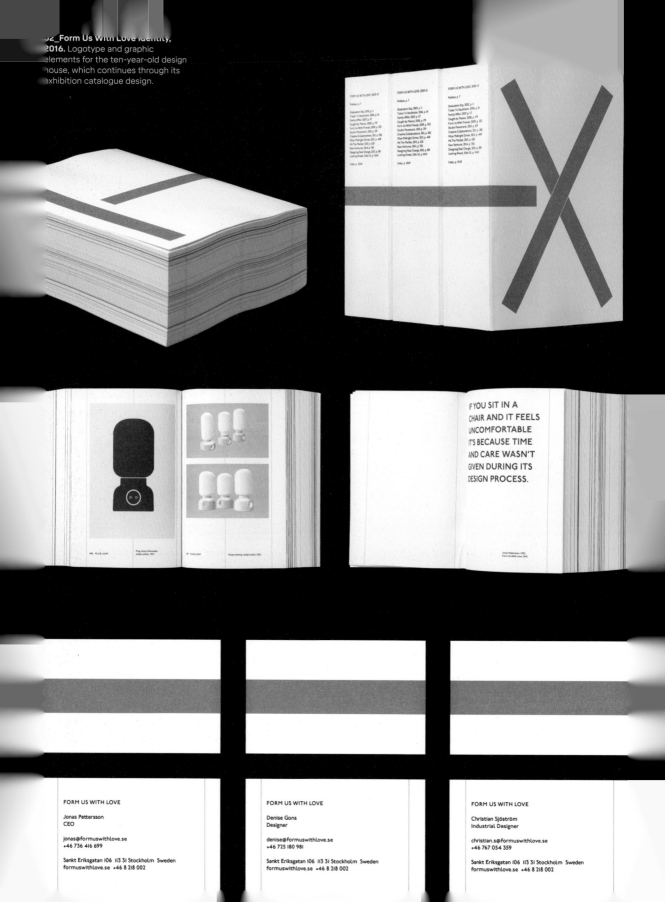

**02_Form Us With Love Identity, 2016.** Logotype and graphic elements for the ten-year-old design house, which continues through its exhibition catalogue design.

IF YOU SIT IN A CHAIR AND IT FEELS UNCOMFORTABLE IT'S BECAUSE TIME AND CARE WASN'T GIVEN DURING ITS DESIGN PROCESS.

FORM US WITH LOVE

Jonas Pettersson
CEO

jonas@formuswithlove.se
+46 736 416 699

Sankt Eriksgatan 106  113 31 Stockholm  Sweden
formuswithlove.se  +46 8 218 002

FORM US WITH LOVE

Denise Gons
Designer

denise@formuswithlove.se
+46 725 180 981

Sankt Eriksgatan 106  113 31 Stockholm  Sweden
formuswithlove.se  +46 8 218 002

FORM US WITH LOVE

Christian Sjöström
Industrial Designer

christian.s@formuswithlove.se
+46 767 054 359

Sankt Eriksgatan 106  113 31 Stockholm  Sweden
formuswithlove.se  +46 8 218 002

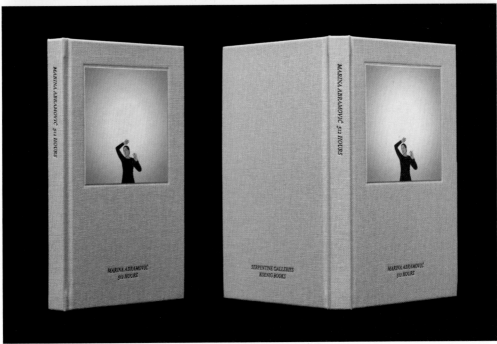

**03_Etel Adnan: The Weight of The World, 2016.** Book design for Etel Adnan's exhibition at the Serpentine Galleries in London.

**04_Marina Abramović: 512 Hours, 2014.** Book design for Marina Abramović's exhibition at the Serpentine Galleries in London.

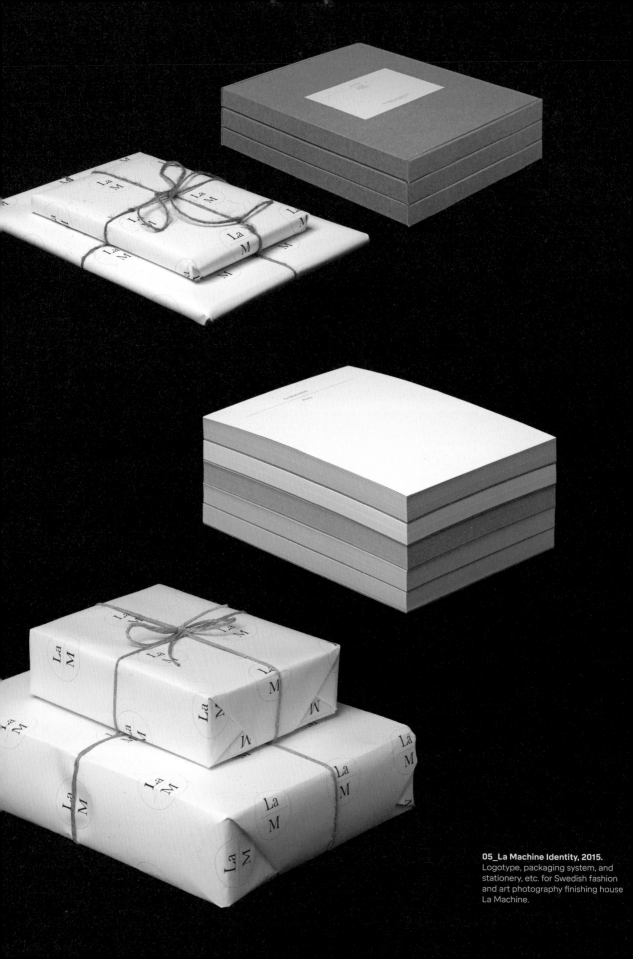

**05_La Machine Identity, 2015.**
Logotype, packaging system, and
stationery, etc. for Swedish fashion
and art photography finishing house
La Machine.

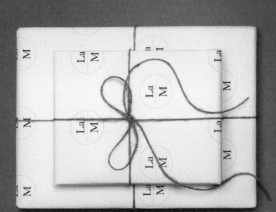

"Everything and nothing inspires me. Music,
conversations, literature, colours and travels.
It's never just one thing, but a whole chain of
associations and collective experiences."

**06_Ingegerd Råman: It's Nothing, but it's
Still Something, 2015.** Book design created
to coincide with the launch of the Swedish
designer's glassware collection commissioned

**07_Olle Eksell — Of Course!, 2015.**
Book design as a tribute to the late
Swedish designer and illustrator's
work, to accompany the launch of
IKEA's ÖNSKEDRÖM collection.

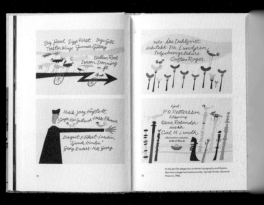

Möt vardagen
med ett leende

**08_ÖNSKEDRÖM collection, 2015.**
Pattern design for carpet, pillow
case, fabrics, etc. using Olle Eksell's
illustrations for IKEA of Sweden.

HENRIK NYGREN DESIGN —— 120/121

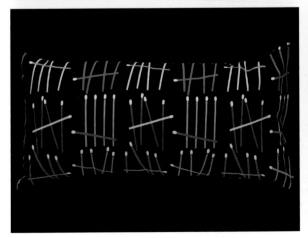

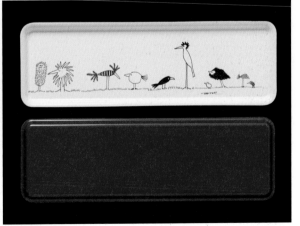

With a mission to create original and innovative products through simple and contemporary designs, Normann Copenhagen challenges conventional thinking and finds the extraordinary in the ordinary. An internationally renowned, award-winning brand by Jan Andersen and Poul Madsen, their diverse and growing collection of furniture, lighting, textiles and home accessories continue to withstand the test of time since its inception in 1999.

# Normann Copenhagen

**01_Ace, 2016.** Lounge sofa and chair design by Hans Hornemann for Normann Copenhagen.

"Imagine a box with a handle
that you simply grab and take
home from the shop and, within
a few minutes, it transforms into
an exclusive lounge chair."
–
NORMANN COPENHAGEN

**02_Ace Chair, 2016.** A lounge collection that unifies upholstered furniture with functional flat-pack principles by Hans Hornemann for Normann Copenhagen.

**03_Era, 2014.** Lounge collection and furniture design by Simon Legald for Normann Copenhagen.

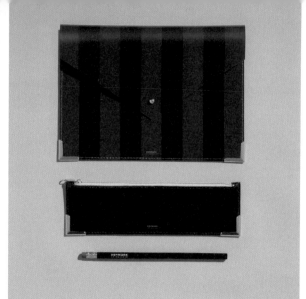

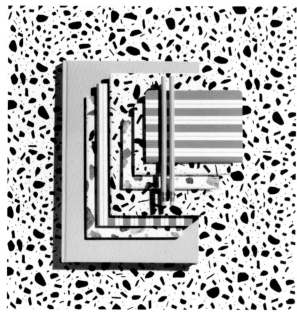
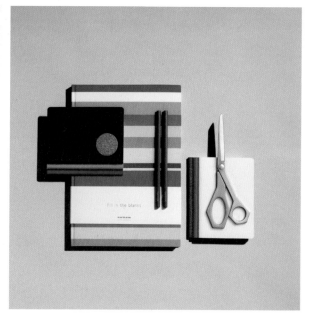

**04_Daily Fiction, 2016.** Stationery design stressing colour combinations, materiality and print by Femmes Régionales for Normann Copenhagen.

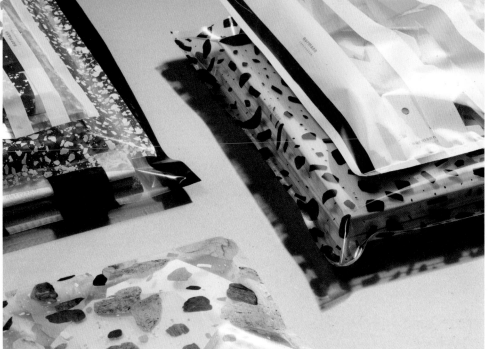

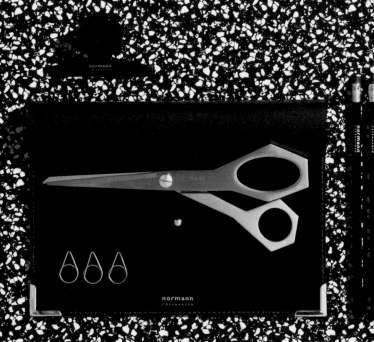

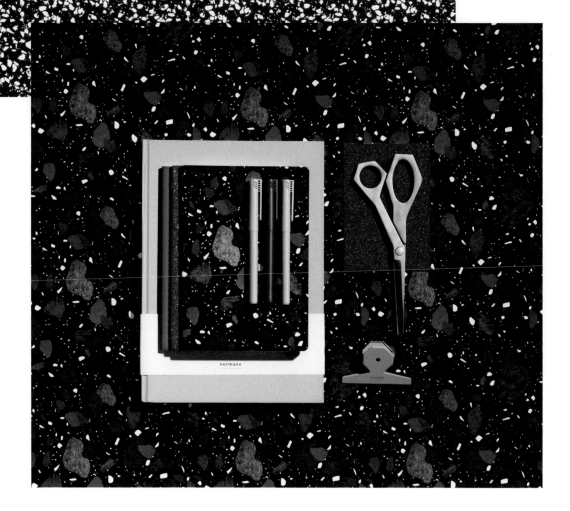

Clara von Zweigbergk uses her breadth of experience at advertising agencies and design studios to create brands, products and art directions committed to simplicity, balance and clean structures. Professionally trained in design and illustration, her intuitive aesthetic sensibility manifests itself in her collaborations with Danish store, HAY. The Stockholm native has also worked with brands such as Nike and Hugo Boss, with an approach united by a passion in paper, colours, typography and forms.

**Copenhagen, Denmark**

• art direction • graphics
• product design

# Clara von Zweigbergk Design

**01_Kaleido Tray, 2012.** Metal tray design launched by furniture design and production brand HAY.

**02_HAY Catalogues, 2010-.** Art direction, graphic design and photo art direction for furniture design and production brand HAY's catalogues.

**03_HAY Brand System, 2010.**
Visual identity, stationery, packaging and catalogue design for furniture design and production brand HAY.

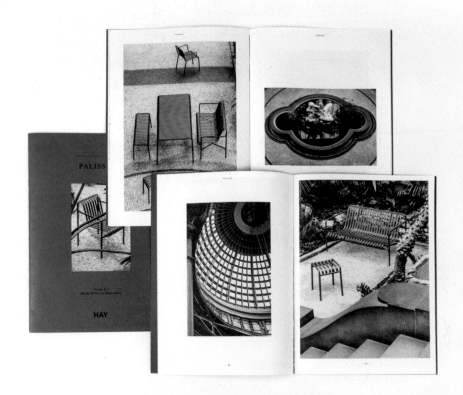

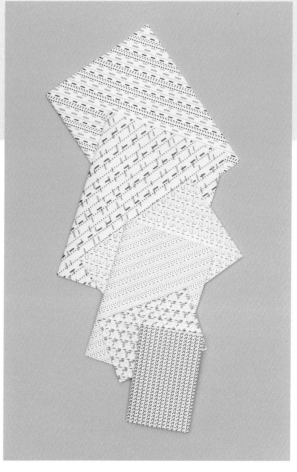

**04_Line Dot Notebook, 2016.**
Design for a notebook set launched
by furniture design and production
brand HAY.

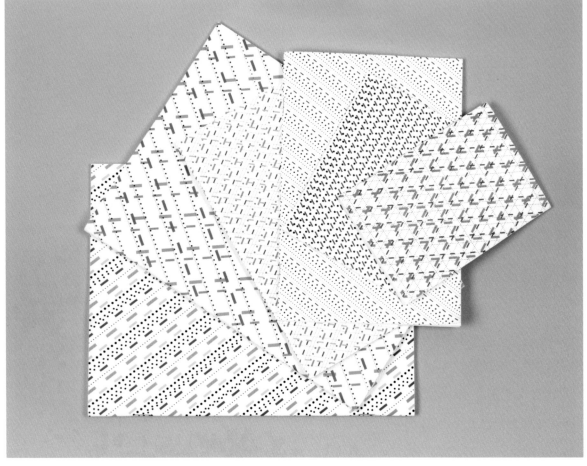

**05_Color Puzzle, 2016.** Wooden puzzle design, launched by gift and home accessories brand Areaware.

**06_Cirque Lamp, 2016.** Lamp design launched by lighting brand Louis Poulsen at the Stockholm Furniture Fair 2016.

# "The combination of an appealing aesthetic and good function is key. Whether it can survive over time is the ultimate test."

–

## CLARA VON ZWEIGBERGK DESIGN

Full interview on page 143

**07_Strike Matchboxes, 2013.** Matchbox collection designed with Shane Schneck, launched by furniture design and production brand HAY.

STOCKHOLM
/SWEDEN

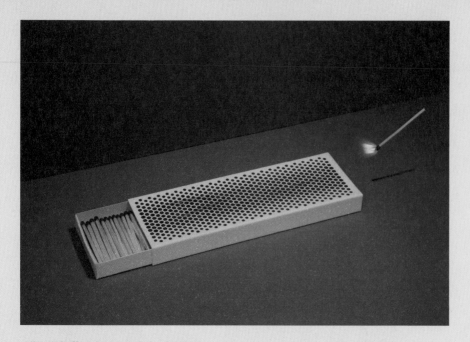

### What define(s) good design?

The combination of an appealing aesthetic and good function is key. Whether it can survive over time is the ultimate test.

Personally I also value design that are directed to a larger audience, meaning it can be afforded and appreciated by a large number of people.

### What was your vision when you started your practice?

Coming mostly from graphic design and art direction, I was inspired by my years in Milan, working at Piero Lissoni's studio and collaborating with industrial designers. Wanting to get more into product design, I worked with Artecnica in Los Angeles on a series of paper mobiles called 'Themis Mobile'. That was my first 3D design in production. At that time I was also asked by HAY to do their new catalogue and art direct the photos. That led to a close collaboration on their visual identity as well as their products.

Many of my products are basically a soft transition from two- to three-dimensional work, but as I learn more about industrial design, I am curious to try new materials and techniques. That's one of the things I love the most with designing products. Each time you are placed in front of new challenges, such as producing something for a reasonable price without compromising the design.

### How would you describe your creative style?

I have a passion for colour and paper, which probably shine through most of my work. I also like symmetry, grids and order (to upweight the lack of it in my life), creating series and objects you can interact with.

**What draw(s) you to stay in Sweden to work?**

My family is based in Stockholm, and that was the main reason I returned here to open my studio.

Work-wise, the world is so open now it matters less where you are based. I work mostly with Danes and Americans at the moment. You can resolve almost anything over e-mail combined with a few trips and Skype calls.

**What are your biggest influences? How do they work their way into your creations?**

These days we are overwhelmed by images, and it is hard to tell where you have seen what, and what has influenced a certain thought. Nature though is a good source of inspiration for me.

I rarely just wake up with an idea. Ideas appear while working, and aren't necessarily related to the current projects. One thing often leads to another.

**How do you ensure ideas/messages can be communicated effectively through your work?**

When working on visual identities, the main task, of course, is to communicate the company's essence and ambitions. Be it a start-up or one wanting a rebrand, it is an interesting part of the process to establish what that's about.

**Can you name one thing that people normally would mistake and one thing people should know about the "Nordic style"?**

I am not so into labels as such. I hope we can all be international designers and the origin of design matters less. And that whoever appreciates it should be able to access it.

**Any upcoming projects?**

I am working on textiles and knitting at the moment, as well as more lighting.

**Strike Matchboxes, 2013**
A tribute to safety matches with a red phosphorus striking surface, a Swedish invention, created in hands with Shane Schneck for HAY.

# CLARA VON ZWEIGBERGK DESIGN

## TEAM

**Clara von Zweigbergk**
Founder & Designer

Sustainability, quality and beauty are Studio Joanna Laajisto's guiding values. Founded in 2010, the boutique design agency creates beautiful, long-lasting and meaningful products and interiors that attach importance to functionality, user experience and clients' needs. Working within the fields of retail and hospitality, for clients from Finland and beyond, the studio's work is internationally recognised by awards and press in the industry.

# Studio
# Joanna Laajisto

**01_Lundia System, 2014.**
Shelving system with box sizes measured by paper size standards for Lundia Oy. Photos by Mikko Ryhänen.

**02_Jackie, 2017.** Bar interior and furniture design for Straight No Chaser Oy. Photos by Mikko Ryhänen.

"We believe that a
well-designed project
is the best form
of sustainability. Our
designs are always crafted
from the end-user's point
of view."
-

STUDIO JOANNA LAAJISTO

**03_MI.NO, 2017.** Retail and interior design for MI.NO, a small show boutique for women's shoes and accessories. Photos by Mikko Ryhänen.

**04_Fjord Helsinki, 2017.** Office and studio interiors for creative agency Fjord Helsinki. Photos by Mikko Ryhänen.

When Swedish word 'Verklig (real, genuine)' combines with German word 'Werk (work)', they become Werklig, an independent Finnish brand agency dedicated to creating great, down-to-earth brand solutions. No simple descriptions can outline Werklig's creative approach, which fosters the team's belief in firm reasoning, co-creation, and the power of branding with a clear purpose. Werklig is recently rebranding the City of Helsinki.

# Werklig

**01_In Search of the Present, 2016.** Graphic identity and editorial design for an exhibition at EMMA Museum that addressed questions which people face in modern times.

VICTOR VASARELY/
OPTISIA MAALAUKSIA/
OPTICAL PAINTINGS/
8.10.2014 – 11.1.2015

**02_Optical Paintings, 2014.** Visual identity and art direction for a Victor Vasarely exhibition at EMMA Museum.

**03_Keisari Bakery, 2015.** New visual identity to coincide with the bakery's name change.

Keisarin leivät ovat leivottu rakkaudella ja intohimolla.
Jokainen leipä on käsintehty ja ammattitaidolla
valmistettu puhtaista ja korkealaatuisista raaka-aineista.
Maista ja rakastu.

Keisaris bröd är tillverkade med kärlek och passion.
Vi använder enbart naturliga och högklassiga råvaror och
varje bröd är bakat för hand av våra yrkeskunniga bagare.
Smaka och bli förälskad.

www.keisari.com

**Pistrina Oy Ab**
Sörnäisten rantatie 33, 00500 Helsinki
Sörnäs strandväg 33, 00500 Helsingfors
09-684 1160

**04_Susanna Vento (Print), 2015.**
Visual identity, packaging and
typeface design for interior stylist
Susanna Vento.

# Wallhanging: #Flowers 03, Around-table.

**05_Susanna Vento (Website), 2015.** Website design to convey Susanna Vento's versatile skill set as an interior stylist.

Susanna Vento, Interior stylist
susanna@susannavento.fi, +358 50 592 0939
Merimiehenkatu 12 a 4, 00150 Helsinki Finland
www.susannavento.fi

**06_Suomen Jäätelö, 2017.** Brand
strategy and packaging for Finnish
ice cream brand Suomen Jäätelö.

WERKLIG —— 162/163

Research and strategic thinking form the basis of 25AH's creative work. The multidisciplinary design agency, or art house, artfully crafts brands and reveals their innate personalities with a sense of nuance. With a notion to create emotional connections, the team uses commercial strategies to tell engaging stories. From types to materials, all elements work to consolidate nuggets and evoke brand environments to be remembered by experience.

**Stockholm, Sweden**

• branding • graphics

# 25AH

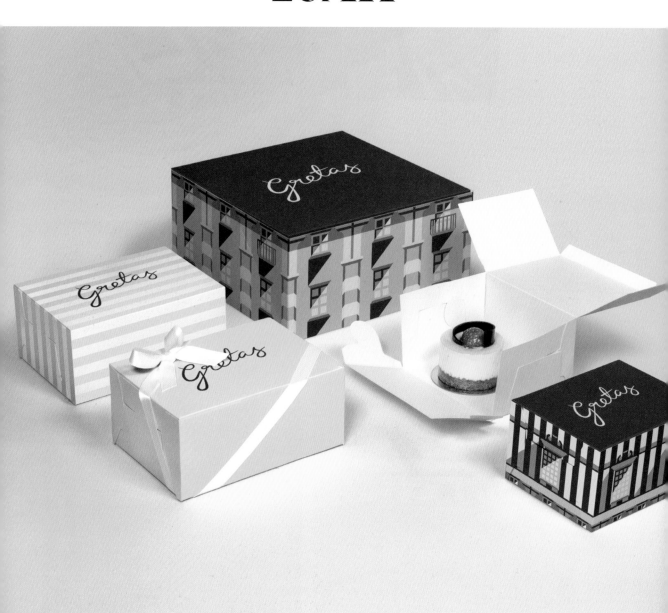

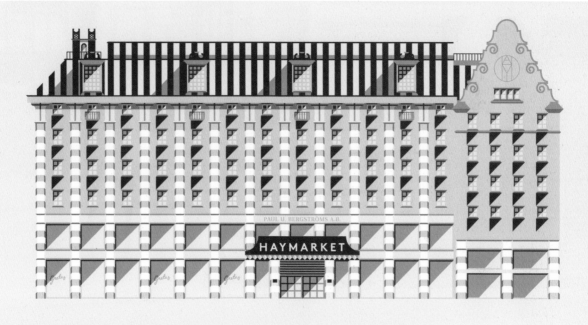

**01_Gretas Café, 2016.** Visual identity and packaging for Stockholm café Gretas.

**02_Café Å Lait, 2014.** Visual identity and packaging for Café Å Lait, a food and beverage concept by Swedish department store Åhléns.

**03_Bonbon Chocolate, 2015.** Self-initiated Christmas gift packaging design developed in collaboration with Swedish chocolatier Chokladfabriken.

**04_Trattoria Montanari, 2015.**
Visual identity and stationery
design for family-run Italian
restaurant Trattoria Montanari
in Stockholm.

**05_Restaurant Grodan, 2016.**
Visual identity and packaging
for brasserie and bar Restaurant
Grodan.

MIXA
&
MATCH FÖR 2
299:-

**06_Åhléns Hem, 2015.** Environmental branding for Swedish department store chain Åhléns.

25AH —— 170/171

**07_Klarna HQ, 2014.** Environmental branding for the headquarters of
e-commerce company Klarna.

25AH —— 172/173

Born in 1979 in Enköping, Sweden, Håkan Ängquist obtained a master's in graphic design at the Konstfack in Stockholm, where he stayed to start a career in design. Before freelancing, Ängquist honed his skills at Henrik Nygren Design and Carl Johan Hane's studio, and has since been developing identities, digital contents and catalogues for cultural institutions and firms. He's currently art directing Design House Stockholm's visual concepts and communications on multiple platforms.

# Håkan Ängquist

**01_16 News Catalogue, 2016.**
Exhibition catalogue showcasing Swedish design manufacturer Design House Stockholm's 2016 product line. Photo & styling by Jonas Lindström Studio.

**02_16 News Exhibition, 2016.** Art direction, graphics, and exhibition design for Design House Stockholm. Photo & styling by Jonas Lindström Studio. Close-up of shelves by Miki Anagrius.

**03_Design House Stockholm 25th Year Anniversary Campaign, 2017.** Custom set design by stylists Sara Garanty, Saša Antić, Synnöve Mork, Tina Hellberg, and Amanda Rodriguez (anticlockwise from left page) at Stockholm's Nordiska Kompaniet department store. Photos by Erik Lefvander.

**04_Design House Stockholm (Snow) Fall Catalogue, 2016.** Art direction and design for the manufacturer's fashion accessories collection. Photos & styling by Jonas Lindström Studio.

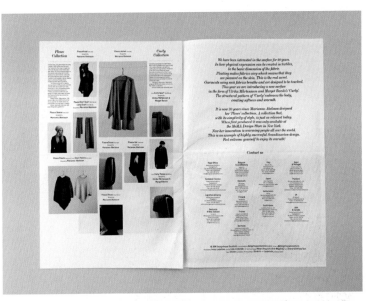

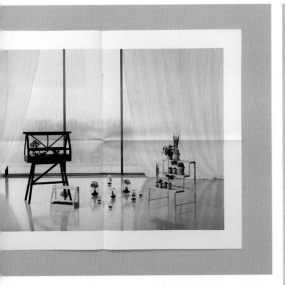

### Trancher
### Cutting board
*by Stig Ahlström*

An elegantly constructed kitchen tool. The board is made of laminated bamboo which is a durable material that can be reground numerous times. The board rests on a silicon ring making it a stable surface for chopping. An indented melamine ring catches meat juices when carving, which makes it easy to pour them into a pan for making a gravy. The melamine ring can also be used for serving vegetables or crisps with a dipping bowl at the centre. And the cutting board is highly suitable for serving cheese and cooked meats.

### Spin Kitchenware
*by Marie-Louise Hellgren*

Marie-Louise Hellgren is the designer responsible for *Höganäs'* highly popular ceramic mugs on a wooden base, as well as for our classic *Spin* mug which she designed nearly ten years ago. Based on the *Spin* design she has created a series of ovenproof stoneware dishes, and bowls. The bowls and dishes are microwave and dishwasher safe.

Included in the *Spin* collection are gratin dishes, pie dishes, soup bowls, ramekins, trays and the original mug. Additional bamboo handles are available that can be used instead of oven gloves when handling hot dishes.

After graduating from HDK, the School of Design and Crafts in Gothenburg, Marie-Louise studied at the *Orrefors Glass School* and the *Pilchuck Glass School in the USA*. Her design is represented at the *Röhsska Museum* in Gothenburg with her stoneware collection designed for *Boda Nova*.

### Timo Tumbler
*by Timo Sarpaneva*

Timo Sarpaneva, one of Finland's most prominent designers, called the *Timo* tumbler his finest glass ever. Made of heat-resistant glass, shaped to fit both big and small hands, and with a slightly cone-shaped top to protect the glass in the dishwasher. The *Timo* tumbler is an excellent example of how form follows function.

*Timo Termo* has an added silicone string that protects the hand. Use it for really hot beverages like tea or coffee.

Professor Timo Sarpaneva was one of Finland's most well-known industrial designers and artists, renowned for his textile and glass products. Timo's work can be found in numerous around the world, including the Museum of Modern Art in New York. He is versatile in his work as a designer and artist, making use of ceramics, metal, textiles, steel and glass in his projects — though glass is probably the material closest to his heart.

**05_Design House Stockholm
2017 Catalogues, 2017.** Oversized catalogues presenting the manufacturer's 2017 collection on various themes. Styling by Saša Antić. Photos by Jonas Lindström Studio.

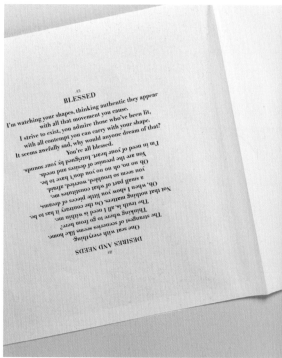

BLESSED

I'm watching your shapes, thinking authentic they appear
with all that movement you cause.
I strive to exist, you admire those who've been lit,
with all contempt you can carry with your shape.
It seems awfully sad, why would anyone dream of that?
You're all blessed.
I'm in need of your heart, intrigued by your sounds.
You are the premise of desires and needs.
Oh no, oh no, oh no, you don't have to be,
you seem so troubled, worried, afraid,
a small part of what constitutes me.
Oh, when I show you little pieces of dreams.
Not that nothing matters. On the contrary it has to be.
The truth is, all I need is within me.
Thinking where to go from here?
The strangest of sceneries seems like home.
One seat with everything.

DESIRES AND NEEDS

**06_The True Bypass — No Hero Sound, 2013.** 12" vinyl and CD packaging and artwork exploring love and lost, and the wonders and despair in the ordinary.

STOCKHOLM
/SWEDEN

**What define(s) good design?**

Good design is not enough. Great design is the ultimate goal. Something extraordinary. Something relevant and beautiful. It's as much about functionality and context as the look and aesthetics.

**What was your vision when you started your practice?**

We envisioned a multidisciplinary approach to design, where everything communicates. We maintain the ambition to make a change.

**How would you describe your creative style?**

They are highly ambitious and hopefully congenial sometimes. Our approach is rooted in the context and a sensibility to solve a problem.

**What draw(s) you to stay in Sweden to work?**

Despite the long dark winter, Sweden is a beautiful and decent country to live in. Even though it's small, we are privileged to work all around the world with clients that give us a broader perspective of design.

Words like "Democratic Design" from IKEA and "Skönhet för alla (Beauty for all)" from the book by Ellen Key in 1899 could on one level affect people's perception of design. Even though we are a country with nine million people, there are 34 interior magazines, weekly interior programmes on each TV channel, too many design blogs and a local radio programme that discusses typography. So design is very exposed, albeit in a very shallow way. On the other hand, Stockholm is also described as a test market with a lot of early adopters.

**What are your biggest influences? How do they work their way into your creations?**

Art has always been a major source of inspiration. We are fuelled by curiosity and love to work on new assignments that we know nothing of. Our solutions and ideas stem from research and insights, mixed with intuition and experience.

Multidisciplinary icons such as Charles and Ray Eames, Massimo Vignelli, Alvar Aalto still inspire us today. But new technology changes our perception everyday of what a holistic brand is or can be.

**How do you ensure ideas/messages can be communicated effectively through your work?**

By being true to a solid process, your ambition and a strong idea. A solid foundation and principles also act as guidance that we can always refer to while creating.

**Can you name one thing that people normally would mistake and one thing people should know about the "Nordic style"?**

Nordic designs are not equivalent to minimalism. Dig deeper into each design's story and you will know.

**Any upcoming projects?**

We're currently working to rebrand Ericsson, The Nobel Prize, Volvo, Polestar, The City of Malmö and Korean fast food brand Hansot; a monospaced version of our own typeface Lab grotesque; packaging for Spendrups beer and a premium liquor brand in China, and many digital start-ups that have to be evaluated.

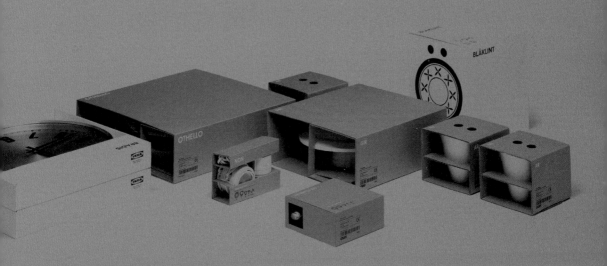

**IKEA Food, 2005-15**
Packaging design incorporating IKEA's philosophy — simplicity, clarity, consistency — and a sprinkling of wit into IKEA's growing Food range.

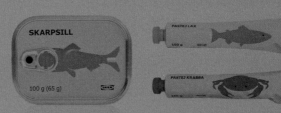

# STOCKHOLM DESIGN LAB

## TEAM

**Björn Kusoffsky**
Founder, CEO & Creative
Director

**Anneli Myrin-Holloway**
COO & Client Director

**Ted Carlström, Eva Dieker**
Account Directors

**Nina Granath**
Creative Director

**Greg Brown**
Digital Director

**Camilla Nilsson, Dennis Friberg**
Project Managers

**Helene Löfgren**
Finance Manager

**Karin Blomberg, Elsa Kusoffsky**
Brand Strategists

**Fredrik Neppelberg,
Per Carlsson**
Senior Designers

**Lukas Nässil, Anna Poijo,
István Vasil, Oscar Gardö,
Magnus Engström**
Designers

Originally from Sweden, Nicklas Hellborg is a multidisciplinary graphic designer and art director currently based in Oslo. With a background in graphic production, Hellborg has hands-on experience in advertising, visual communication and design, working at top agencies such as Neumeister, DDB Stockholm and Motherland. The creative individual now collaborates with SMFB and APT, and has played a key role in IKEA Norway's campaigns since 2011.

# Nicklas Hellborg

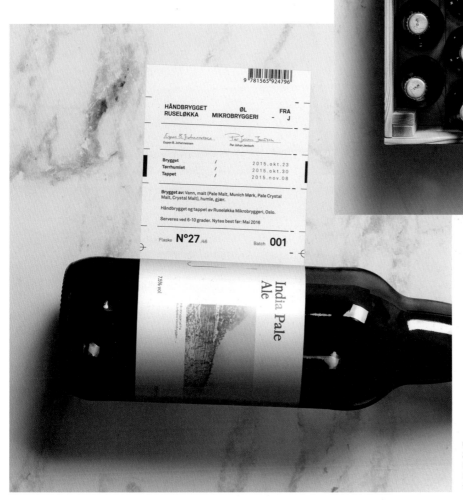

**01_Ruseløkka Microbrewery, 2016.** Packaging for a small brewery's first batch of craft beer as Christmas gifts for the founders' family and friends.

**02_IKONIC Apparel, 2016.**
Brand identity for a fashion distributor which manages the sales of Neuw Denim, Human Scales and Fred Perry in Norway.

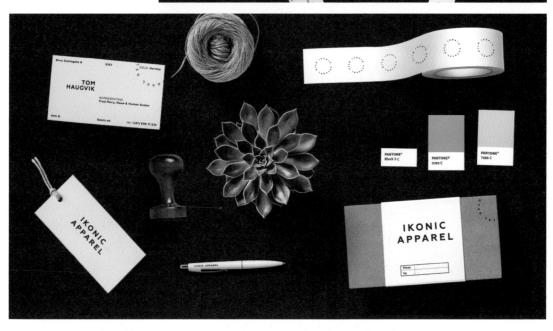

PANTONE®
7486 C

PANTONE®
Black 3 C

PA
33

PANTONE®
3385 C

PA
748

**03_NJORD Organic Restaurant, 2016.** Brand identity for a restaurant concept that offers an affordable "New Nordic" menu fed with seasonal, organic products.

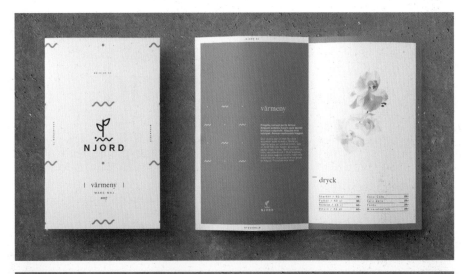

With a diverse team of experts, Bond offers brand solutions that put graphic, digital, spatial, and words to good use. With attention to craftsmanship and artistic details, the team helps crystallise visions and mature growth for new and established brands. Created in Helsinki in 2009 by Jesper Bange, Aleksi Hautamäki and Arttu Salovaara, Bond takes great pride in being founded and run entirely by designers. Their offices in London and Abu Dhabi blend local influences with Bond's Nordic reasoning.

# Bond Creative Agency

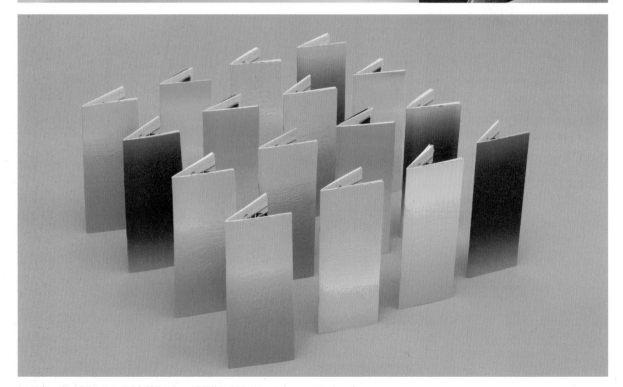

**01_University of the Arts Helsinki Brochure, 2013.** Individual brochure cover designs for the new university created in hands with DMP printing house, using Iris prints.

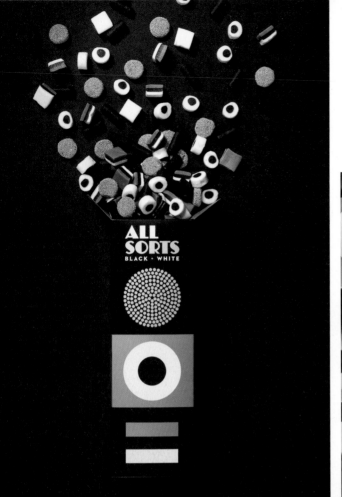

**02_Allsorts Black and White, 2016.**
Packaging for confectionery maker
Cloetta's liquorice, reflecting the
colourless sweet content.

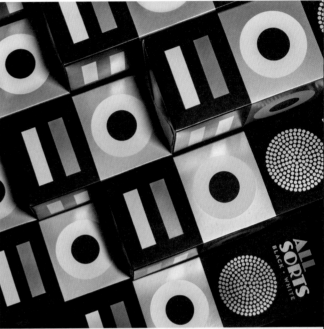

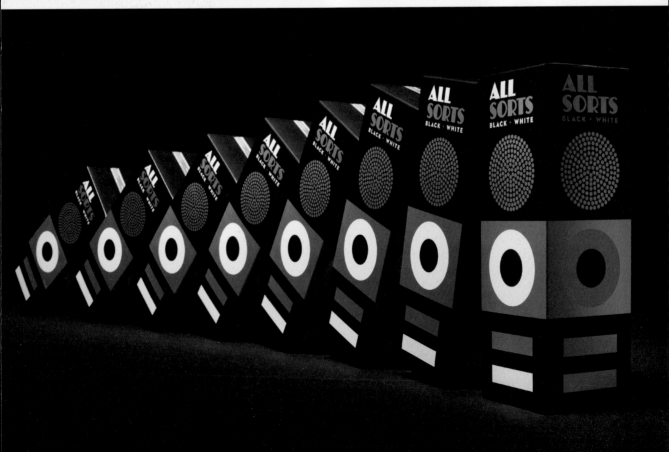

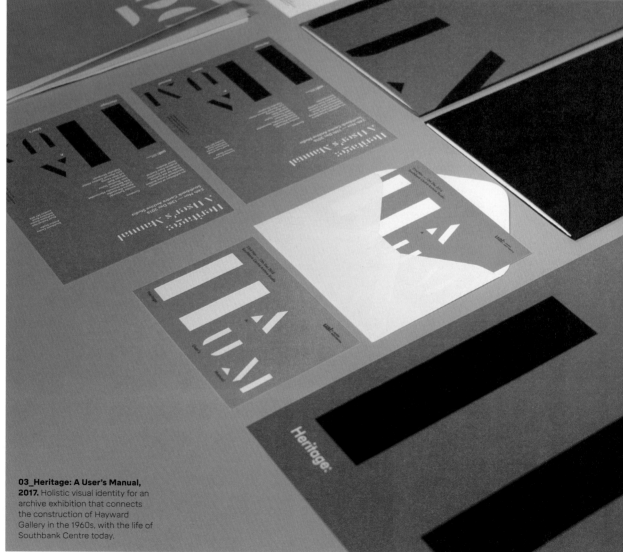

**03_Heritage: A User's Manual, 2017.** Holistic visual identity for an archive exhibition that connects the construction of Hayward Gallery in the 1960s, with the life of Southbank Centre today.

**04_Heritage: A User's Manual (Typography), 2017.** Stencil type representing the mix of architectural elements and archival material from different eras presented in the exhibition.

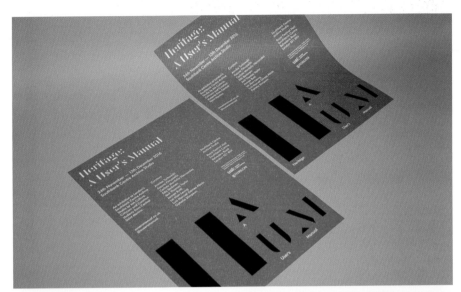

**05_Well Coffee (Branding), 2016.**
Visual identity and digital design for
a new vegetarian café, featuring a
stylised typeface and a pale blue to
correspond with the name.

WELL
MADE
ORGANIC
COFFEE

**06_Well Coffee (Interiors), 2016.**
Signage and spatial design for a
new vegetarian café based around
a wave concept.

## WELL, HERE'S OUR MENU

| | | | | | |
|---|---|---|---|---|---|
| DEATH BEFORE DECAF | | | LATTE | 4,50 | 5,50 |
| DARK ROAST | 2,70_ | | BUTTER COFFEE | 3,50 | |
| ESPRESSO | 2,90 | 3,40 | TEA | 2,50 | |
| AMERICANO | 3,00 | | MATCHA LATTE | 4,70_ | |
| MACCHIATO | 3,30 | | CHAI LATTE | 4,70_ | |
| CAPPUCCINO | 3,70 | | CACAO | 4,50 | |

**07_Moi Helsinki (Interiors),
2016.** Environmental branding
for a bar inside Helsinki-Vantaa
Airport based upon Helsinki's
varied personalities.

**08_Moi Helsinki (Branding), 2016.** Illustrations and lettering for a bar inside Helsinki-Vantaa Airport across its menus, beer glasses and coasters.

**09_Tilly Sveaas Jewellery Branding, 2016.** Art direction, packaging and web design for a London jeweller.

Parasol's specialties lie in the realm of creative direction. Founded by creative directors Ramiro Oblitas and Saul Taylor, and combining the marketing expertise of Victor Abellan, the creative firm brings together their experiences at industry giants such as *Wallpaper* and *Apartamento* magazines, to build brands with a diverse network that stresses quality, details and determination to succeed. The team works without disciplinary and physical boundaries, from offices in Stockholm, Barcelona and New York City.

Stockholm, Sweden
Barcelona, Spain
New York City, US

• branding • editorial
• digital design

# Parasol

**01_Design Sweden (Art direction), 2016-17.** Exhibition art direction for Design Sweden, launched during the annual Stockholm Design Week. Photos by Anthony Hill and Brendan Austin.

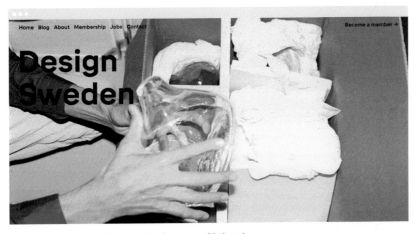

Design Sweden is an organisation set up with the sole

**02_Design Sweden (Web Design), 2016-17.** Web design as part of the rebranding of Design Sweden, made in collaboration with Kod & Form.

**03_Design Sweden (Communications), 2016-17.** Marketing materials and brochure created in collaboration with Letters from Sweden. Photos by Anthony Hill and Brendan Austin.

**Design Sweden
1957 onwards**

You
believe
in
collaboration
between
design
disciplines.

**04_Design Sweden (Rebranding),
2016–17.** Custom typeface designed in
hands with Letters from Sweden, and
stationery for Design Sweden. Photos
by Anthony Hill and Brendan Austin.

Design Sweden
1957 onwards

Ludvig Franzén
Member 1049

Design Sweden
1957 onwards

Ramiro Oblitas
Member 1137

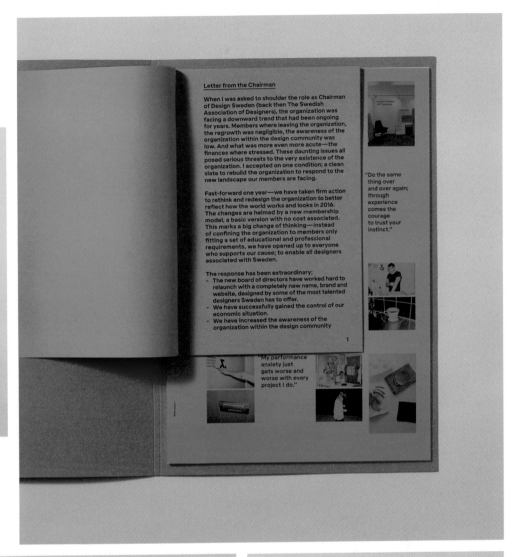

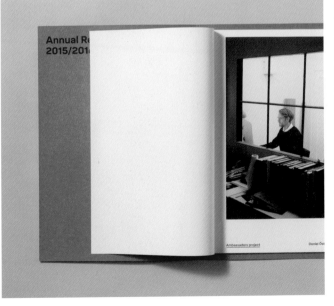

**05_Design Sweden (Book Design), 2016-17.** Year-end review designed as part of Design Sweden's new identity scheme. Photos by Anthony Hill and Brendan Austin.

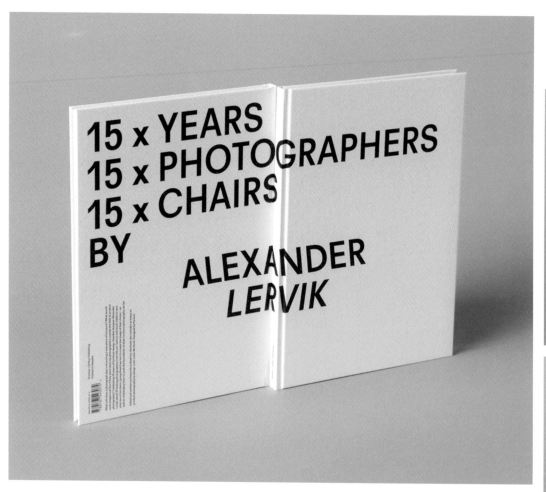

**06_Alexander Lervik, 2014.** Creative direction and publication design that celebrate and document product designer Alexander Lervik's 15 years of work. Photos by Alexander Crispin.

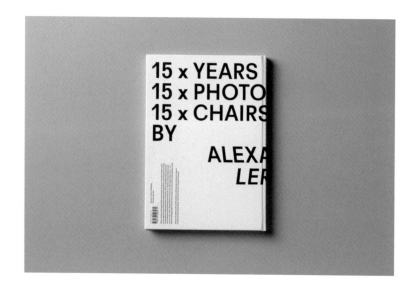

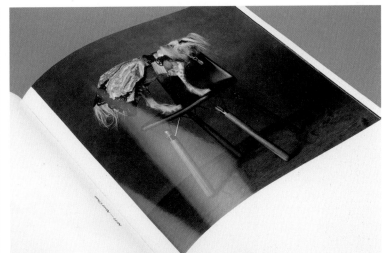

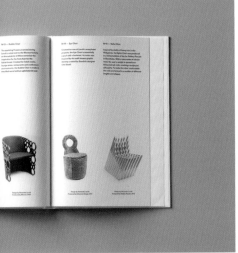

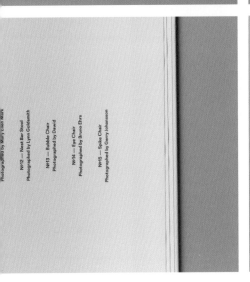

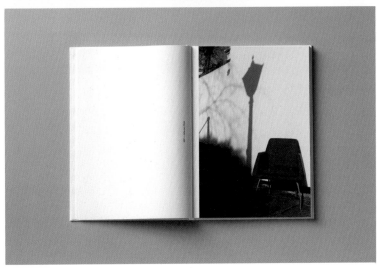

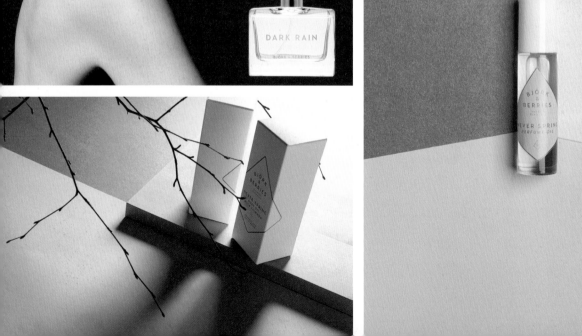

**07_Björk & Berries Brand Image Campaigns, 2012-16.** A brand overhaul to re-position an ecological Scandinavian cosmetics brand. Photos by Ola Bergengren, Brendan Austin, and Alexander Crispin.

**08_Björk & Berries Packaging
& Communications, 2012-16.**
Packaging and marketing collateral
that help define the cosmetics brand's
first perfume category. Photos by
Ola Bergengren, Brendan Austin and
Alexander Crispin.

**09_Björk & Berries Gift Packaging & Communications, 2012-16.** Whole packaging range and communications for seasonal collections and product launches. Photos by Ola Bergengren, Brendan Austin and Alexander Crispin.

PARASOL —— 210/211

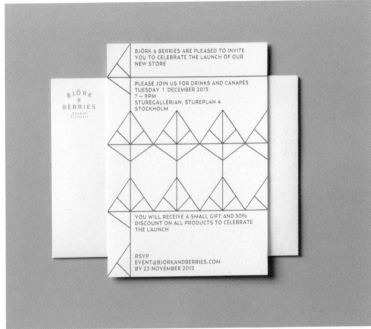

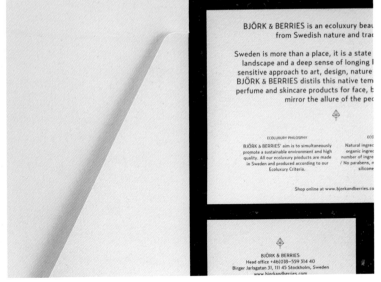

Lou Andrea Savoir
lou@savoirjoaillerie.com
+49-151-252-657-49

Savoir Joaillerie

info@savoirjoaillerie.com
savoirjoaillierie.com

Olivier Talbot/Operations
olivier@savoirjoaillerie.com
+34-664-578-784

Savoir Joaillerie

info@savoirjoaillerie.com
savoirjoaillierie.com

Savoir Joaillerie

Dear Ramiro                    Berlin 11/12
Here are 3 boxes for your perusal.
I'm thinking the complimentary
card and the business card, maybe?
Might all benefit from a color
match in some detail.
As you can see the boxes close
really pretty flush and can be
confusing - it can create pretty →

With Compliments

Savoir Joaillerie

Savoir Joaillerie

925

Savoir Joaille

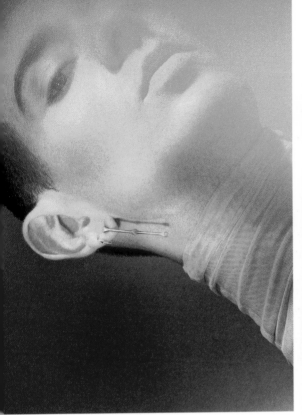

**10_Savoir Joaillerie, 2014-15.**
Visual identity, art direction, and packaging design for jeweller Savoir Joaillerie to enhance sensitivity. Campaign photography by Fredrik Altinell & Trevor Good, courtesy of Savoir Joaillerie. Product shots by Alexander Crispin.

The name 'Neue' is reflective of the design studio's core principle. A cross-disciplinary design studio full of dedicated creatives, experienced consultants and efficient process managers, Neue harnesses the power of contrast and polarisation to create new visual stories using a fresh, relevant and remarkable language. Albeit small, their creative team works to unite the fields of strategy, technology and design and maintain a close relation with their clients.

Oslo, Norway

• advertising • identity
• digital design

# Neue
# Design Studio

**01_Paleet (Branding), 2016.**
Branding strategy, web design, launch campaign, and art direction for new fashion and lifestyle retail brand Paleet.

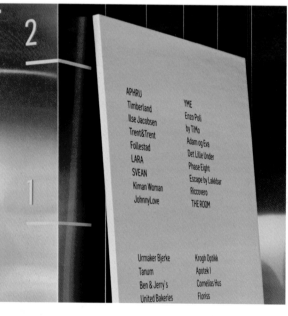

APHRU
Timberland
Ilse Jacobsen
Trent&Trent
Follestad
LARA
SVEAN
Kiman Woman
JohnnyLove

YME
Enzo Poli
by TiMo
Adam og Eva
Det Lille Under
Phase Eight
Escape by Lakkbar
Riccovero
THE ROOM

Urmaker Bjerke
Tanum
Ben & Jerry's
United Bakeries

Krogh Optikk
Apotek 1
Cornelias Hus
Floriss

**02_Paleet (Navigational system), 2016.** A visual universe meant to express Paleet's warm personality and turn the venue into an inspiring destination for fashion and lifestyle goods.

OLIVER DUBOIS

**03_Dansens Hus, 2016.** Visual
identity, typeface based on Dia
from Schick-Toikka, and web design
for Dansens Hus, Norway's national
institute for dance.

THE
JAPANESE
GARDEN

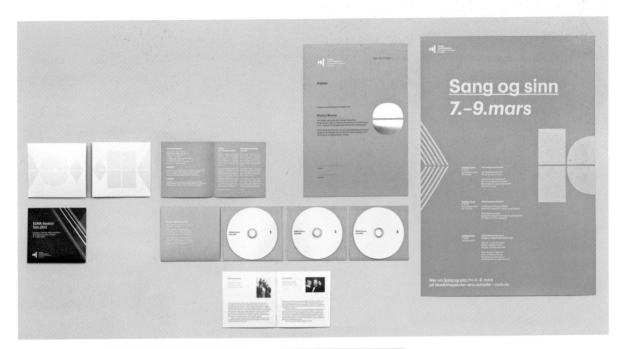

**04_Norwegian Academy of Music, 2015.** Visual identity, web design, art direction, and editorial and publication design for the Academy of Music inspired by sound waves.

**05_Altaskifer, 2015.** Visual identity, web design, editorial, and product design for joint sales and marketing brand Alta Quartzite, representing the slate industry in Alta, Norway.

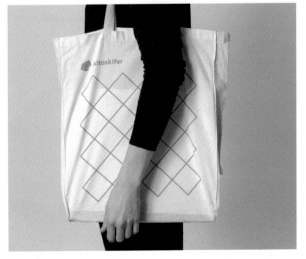

**06_Hegel Music System, 2015.**
Packaging and editorial design for
Hegel Music System using basic
shapes and bold colours.

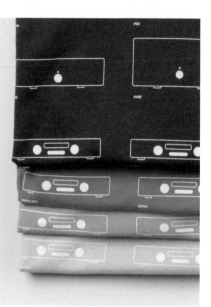

OSLO
/NORWAY

## What define(s) good design?

It should solve a problem, otherwise it's just decoration. Simple, easy to use and lasting — not just adapting to the latest trends. It should be thorough and well crafted regardless of style.

## What was your vision when you started your practice?

We didn't really have a central vision — it came out through the years. But we had confidence in ourselves and believed that we had something new to contribute to the Norwegian design scene. There weren't a lot of studios around at that time that shared our thoughts on design. Since the start we've been fond of keeping our language simple, reducing it as much as necessary, so we've embraced constraints and dogma-like principles.

## How would you describe your creative style?

Idea-based, reduced and crafted. It's hard to describe. It might be more of a mindset than a style.

## What draw(s) you to stay in Norway to work?

Easy access to nature and mountains for hiking and skiing. The seasons are very pronounced so you really feel the change of times throughout the year. Exciting things are happening with start-ups in Norway, and businesses share a positive attitude towards the importance of design.

## What are your biggest influences? How do they work their way into your creations?

It's naturally a complex constellation of influences. We're still inspired by the International Style design movement and all the legendary designers who practised during that time. But lately we get really inspired by creative technology and coding, like, what can be done with openFrameworks, and especially how this can be used to interact directly with people. We also find inspirations in innovative products, be it a physical or digital design.

## How do you ensure ideas/messages can be communicated effectively through your work?

We try to remove anything that might obstruct ideas — and keep only what's essential for it to come through. We like directness and contrasts — we will try to use very few colours or type styles on each surface.

**Can you name one thing that people normally would mistake and one thing people should know about the "Nordic style"?**

Some people mistake it for pure minimalism — which it really isn't. I like to think that we merge simplicity with high contrast and tactility, which is inspired by the nature that surrounds us.

**Any upcoming projects?**

Yes. We're currently finishing up an identity and a website for an English publisher which will function as sort of a publishing platform. We're also working on a news app aiming for young people for Norway's largest newspaper. In addition to that we're working with a lot of Norwegian start-ups, including two working economy/saving-solutions.

## TEAM

**Mathias Haddal Hovet**
Managing Partner

**Pia Winther,**
**Ida Bentsen**
Project Managers

**Stein Henrik Haugen,**
**Thomas Lein,**
**Lars Kjelsnes,**
**Martin Sanne Kristiansen**
Designers & Partners

**Felix Skaara,**
**Simon Gustavsson**
Designers

Founded by Jonas Banker and Ida Wessel, BankerWessel is an award-winning agency with an internationally regarded reputation. Using graphic design as an effective tool, they create long term and memorable solutions for print, digital and spatial contexts. Their design solutions, exhibition graphics and publications are filled with passion, experience and craft, made collaboratively with worldwide clients and receiving both attention and acclaim.

**Stockholm, Sweden**

• identity • graphics • editorial

# BankerWessel

**01_Patrick Demarchelier Exhibition Launch Party Invitation, 2017.** Scarf invitation as a nod to the acclaimed fashion photographer and his work, on display at Fotografiska, a centre for contemporary photography in Stockholm.

**02_Patrick Demarchelier Exhibition Identity, 2017.** Environmental graphics for the celebrated fashion photographer's exhibition at Fotografiska, using black and white and typeface Arcadia, which Neville Brody designed in the 1990s.

**03_Martin Parr Exhibition Identity, 2015.** Typeface and graphic design referencing Martin Parr's beach images for his photo exhibition "Souvenir" at Fotografiska.

**04_Fotografiska Graphic Identity, 2010-.** Graphic
concept and logo design for the independent
cultural venue, Fotografiska (Museet), dedicated to
contemporary photography.

**05_Efter Babel, 2015.** Graphic and publication design for group exhibition "Efter Babel" at Moderna Museet that explores the role of language in contemporary art.

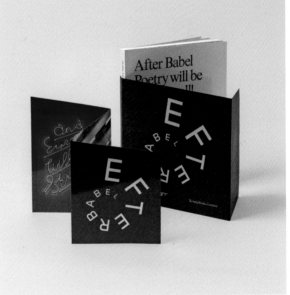

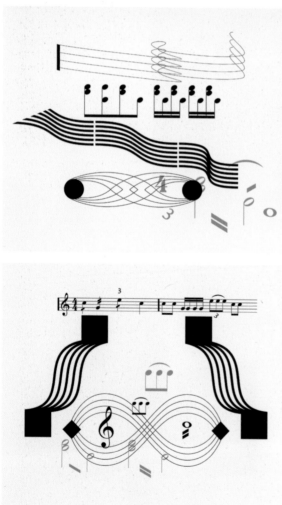

**06_På Scen/On Stage, 2017.** Visual identity for exhibition "På Scen/On Stage" at Scenkonstmuseet, Swedish Museum of Performing Arts.

**07_På Scen/On Stage Signage, 2017.** Visual language graphically conveys interactivity and artistic energy that pervade the "På Scen/On Stage" exhibition at Scenkonstmuseet.

Bedow is a small team of designers with more than a decade of experience working on visual identities, publications, packagings and more. Founder Perniclas Bedow leads the team to create engaging projects outside the norm that are full of colour, energy and their own little quirks, emphasising on clear and durable visual communication. Constantly challenging themselves, the consistent enthusiasm of the award-winning studio is reflected in their work.

**Stockholm, Sweden**

• identity • packaging • interior

# Bedow

**01_Fable Skateboards Visual Identity, 2017.** Logo, character design, and product design for a new skate brand.

**02_Fable Skateboards Illustrations, 2017.** Colour palette, patterns, animations and typography for a new skate brand that aimed at skaters who want to make a difference as they ride.

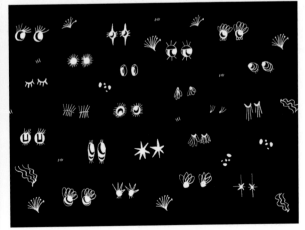

**03_Anna Bjerger (Limited Edition), 2017.** Special edition book design for
the Swedish artist, featuring a signed and numbered box and the artist's
fingerprints running along the book's edges.

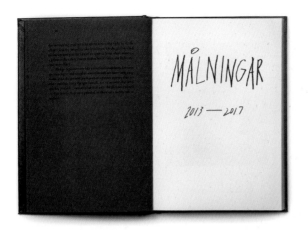

**04_Anna Bjerger Editorial Design, 2017.** Book showcasing the Swedish artist's work between 2013 and 2017 to accompany her exhibition "Familiar Shadows" at Kristianstads Konsthall.

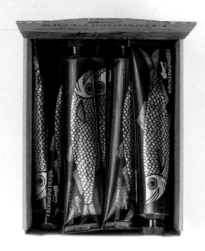

**05_Biggans Böcklingpastej, 2016.**
Packaging for a fish paste made of smoked herring.

# "Dohop's logotype is flexible in the sense that it can communicate things, destinations or people."

—

BEDOW

**06_Dohop Visual Identity, 2016.** Brand strategy, Typeface, brand colours, illustrations, and pictograms for online flight search engine, Dohop.

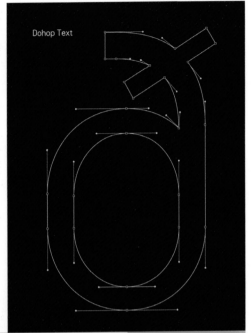

Dohop Text

D O H O P

Anywhere. Simple.

Anywhere. Simple.

Grass

Canola

Beach

Poppy

River

Ocean

**07_It's Time For... LP Packaging, 2016.** Vinyl sleeve design for the limited supply of The Hope Singers' debut album, LP edition, released on the Sing a Song Fighter label.

**08_It's Time For... Visual Identity, 2016.** Custom typeface and illustrations for The Hope Singers debut album LP release.

Through their multi-disciplinary art and design studio, Nan Na Hvass and Sofie Hannibal have worked collaboratively since 2006 to produce various exquisite projects ranging from tactile installation work to illustration, full art direction, and graphic design solutions. Balancing between non-commercial and commercial creations, they keep their minds and hands creatively challenged, and continue to push their limitations within the art.

**Copenhagen, Denmark**

• branding • art direction
• illustration

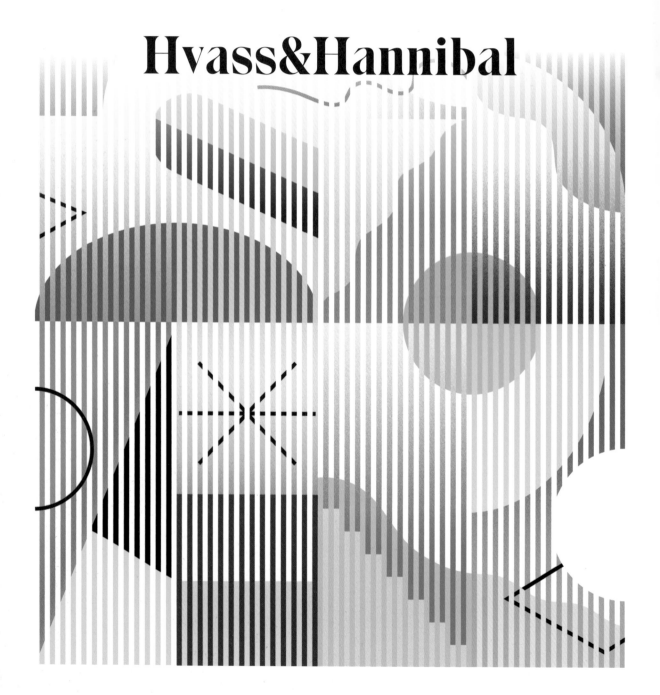

# Hvass&Hannibal

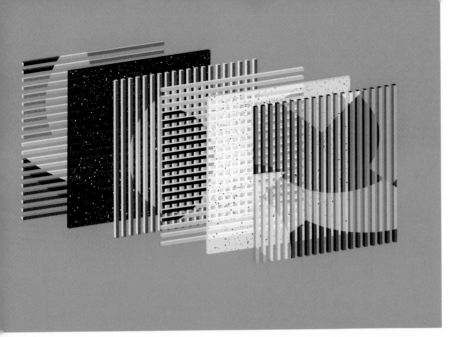

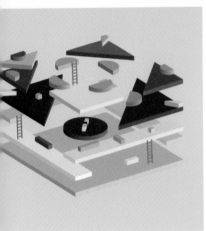

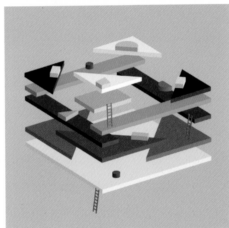

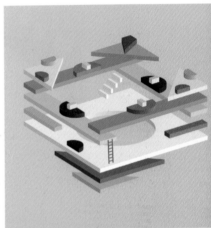

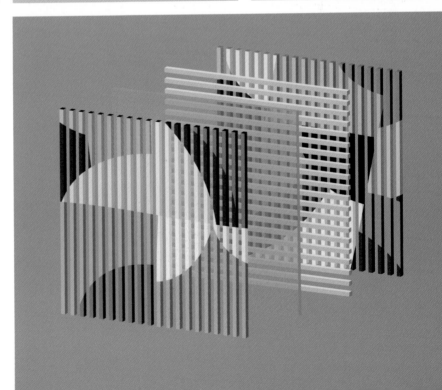

**01_AMV BBDO Murals, 2017.**
Artworks rendered for the interior
of ad-agency AMV BBDO's London
headquarters. Curated and
commissioned by Kirstie Johnstone.

**02_AMV BBDO Installation, 2017.** Murals installed for ad-agency AMV BBDO's London headquarters. Curated and commissioned by Kirstie Johnstone.

**03_Realdania Persona, 2016.** Wood figures and characters representing the people with varied social and ethnic backgrounds which Realdania's philanthropic projects serve. Photos by Helle Sandager.

**04_Biotherm, 2016.** Packaging for Biotherm's special Christmas set. The profit derived from the sales would go to support the work of environmental charity Mission Blue.

HVASS&HANNIBAL —— 248/249

Rejecting traditions and conservative ideas, Snask brings authenticity and charisma to the table. Aiming to challenge industries with vivid creativity and humour, their projects offer a highly distinctive quality by defying the norm, working with confidence between branding, design and film. On top of that, they have a manifesto, a book called "*Make Enemies and Gain Fans*", lecture tours on creative entrepreneurship, and their own record label.

Snask

Multi is the

new regular

**01_#MONKIFESTO**
**Communication Concept & Set**
**Design, 2016.** Typography, banners,
and signs convey ideas of women
empowerment for a Swedish
women's fashion brand's 10th
anniversary campaign. Makeup
& hair by Viktoria Sörensdotter.
Photos by Arvida Byström.

Let love loose

Cut the norm

**02_#MONKIFESTO Statements, 2016.**
Slogans for Swedish women's fashion
label Monki, aiming to take a stand
for women living in different cultures.
Makeup & hair by Viktoria Sörensdotter.
Photos by Arvida Byström.

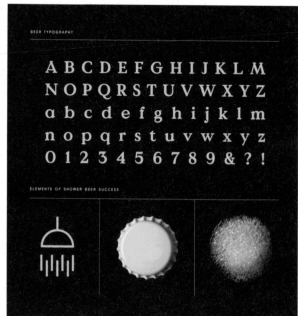

**03_Shower Beer, 2016.** Packaging design for self-initiated beer project made in collaboration with Pangpang Brewery.

**04_Kaibosh (Typeface), 2016.**
Custom display typeface, Sentrum,
matched eyewear brand Kaibosh's
brand tonality.

**05_Kaibosh (Visual Identity), 2016.** Signage, interior fixtures, window decals, typeface, and corporate stationery to channel eyewear brand Kaibosh's boldness and energy throughout their shop.

SNASK —— 256/257

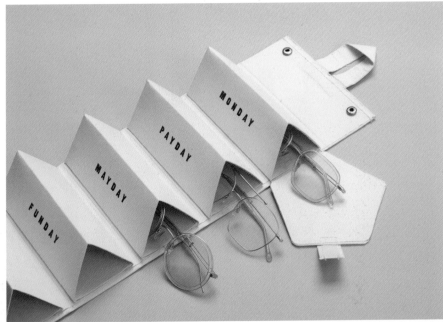

# KAIBOSH
## EYEWEAR
## STORE

**KAIBOSH**

MON-THUR: 10.00-18.00

FRIDAY: 10.00-19.00

SATURDAY: 10.00-16.00

SUNDAY: CLOSED

**06_Kaibosh (Posters), 2016.** Posters created as part of eyewear shop Kaibosh's rebranding campaign.

**07_North Korea, 2016.** Self-initiated rebranding proposal for North Korea. Scheme includes an open letter to the North Korean government, stationery, typeface and more. Art directed by Asta Ostrovskaja.

With offices in Norway and Austria, Bleed works to challenge conventions around art, media and identity. Restless, intuitive and contemplative, founders Svein Haakon Lia and Dag Solhaug Laska let the power of visual language play into visual identities, packaging, interactive design, and art projects, through effective brand strategies, art directions and compelling designs that have won international acclaim. The consultancy's motto, Bleed for the revolution™, articulates of their values.

Oslo, Norway
Vienna, Austria

• identity • experience
• product

# Bleed

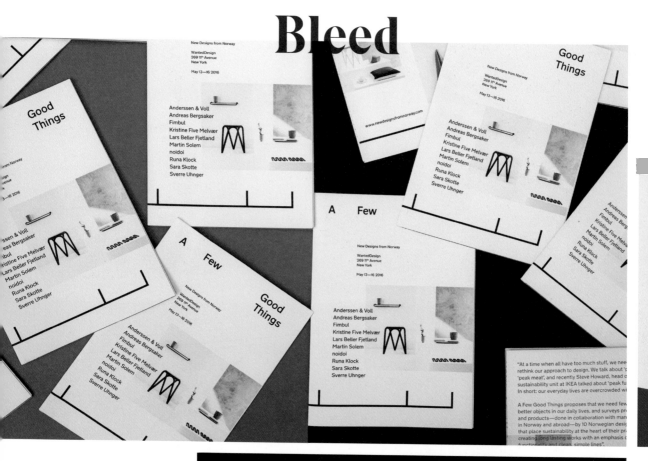

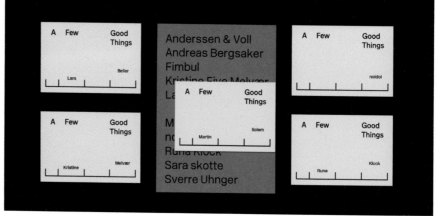

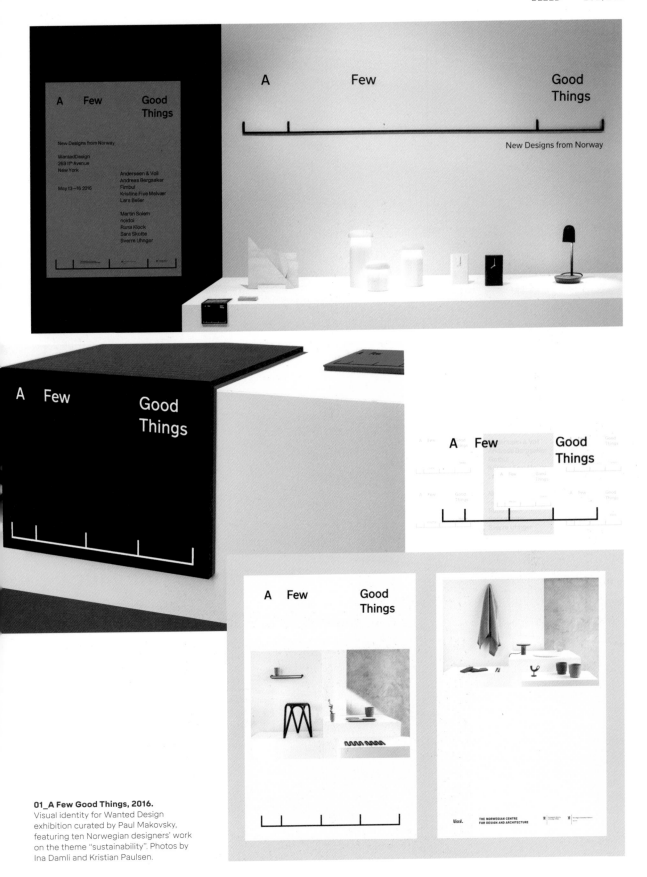

**01_A Few Good Things, 2016.**
Visual identity for Wanted Design
exhibition curated by Paul Makovsky,
featuring ten Norwegian designers' work
on the theme "sustainability". Photos by
Ina Damli and Kristian Paulsen.

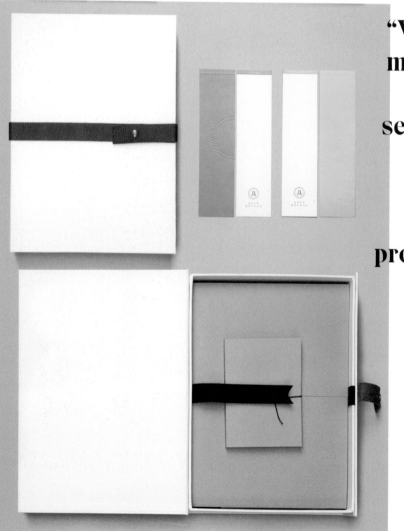

**"What we share is more an approach to challenge the segments we work within. We use a lot of time in the concept phase prototyping ideas."**

–

BLEED

Full interview on page 099

**02_Aker Brygge, 2013.** Visual
identity for a mixed development
on a former shipyard.

Russian architecture group based on idea of perfection and a quote from Irish novelist Samuel Beckett.

**Blank Architects**
Krasnoproletarskaya ul 16C2
Moscow, Russia 127473

Experience
350 projects across the
Russian Federation

Leader
One of the leading
architectural firms in the
Moscow and Russian markets.

Giles Deleuze
and Felix Guattari

01 Find potential movements of
deterritorialization, possible lines of flight.

**Blank Architects**
Krasnoproletarskaya ul 16C2
Moscow, Russia 127473

Experience
350 projects across the
Russian Federation

Leader
One of the leading
architectural firms in the
Moscow and Russian markets.

Albert Einstein

02 Look deep into the nature
and you will understand everthing better.

**Blank Architects**
Krasnoproletarskaya ul 16C2
Moscow, Russia 127473

Experience
350 projects across the
Russian Federation

Leader
One of the leading
architectural firms in the
Moscow and Russian markets.

Albert Einstein

02 Look deep into the nature
and you will understand everthing better.

Concept
V. 2016.12.04

The building as
attraction or obstacle

A.      Attraction
B.      Obstacle

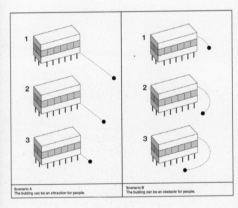

Scenario A
The building can be an attraction for people.

Scenario B
The building can be an obstacle for people.

Blank Architects
Concept and identity
V. 2016.12.04

Concept
V. 2016.12.04

How architecture
affects the pedestrian flow.

1.2.
Cities can be recognized
by their pace just as
people can by their walk

Attachments
Blank Architects Capability Statement

Playtime by Jacques Tati. 1967

Hats in the Garment District by Margaret Bourke White. 1930

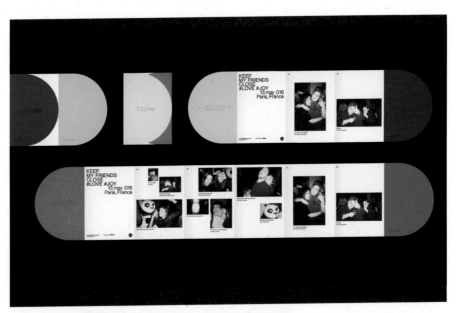

**04_Clicher Graphic Identity, 2016.**
Contemporary approach speaks to French photo-printing firm Clicher's young and creative client base. Photos by Estelle Piguet.

# Clicher

229 Route de Seysses
31100 Toulouse
France

La maison Clicher
ne ressemblera pas simplement
à une belle demeure de magazine.

La maison Clicher
se vibrer de tout son corps

Book now on +33 558563005
01    or visit www.clicher.com

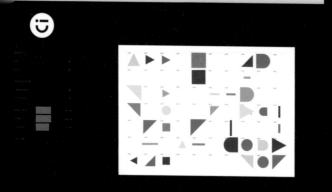

Clicher
Identity

---

Grotesk    Regular

32pt    Le photographe réalise des scènes ou il se met lui même en scène. Il se déguise et se glisse ds la peau de gens qui attendent le bus durant la nuit ou pour une fois.

---

24pt    Le photographe et graphiste réalise des scènes ou il se met lui-même en scène. Il se déguise et se glisse dans la peau de personnages loufoques qui attendent le bus durant la nuit. Pour une fois, il est facile de deviner quelle est la destination de ces perso qui attendent patiemment assis sur

---

Clicher
Identity

---

Grotesk    Regular

22pt    Le photographe et graphiste réalise des scènes humoristiques dans lesquelles il se met lui-même en scène. Il se déguise et se glisse dans la peau de personnages loufoques qui attendent le bus durant la nuit. Pour une fois, il est facile de deviner quelle est la destination de ces personnalités qui attendent patiemment assis sur leur banc. Le photographe et graphiste réalise des scènes humoristiques dans lesquelles il se met lui-même en scène. Il se déguise et se glisse dans la peau de personnages loufoques qui attendent le bus durant la nuit.
Pour une fois, il est facile de deviner quelle est la destination de ces personnalités qui attendent patiemment assis sur leur banc.

---

10pt    J'ai commencé à faire mes propres images en 2010 et n'ai cessé depuis, de passer par de multiples phases. J'essaie un peu tout pour me familiariser avec mon boîtier et trouver la sensible photographique qui me convient le plus. J'ai fini par remporter ce concours au terme d'une belle compétition pleine d'adrénaline et de rebondissements, ce qui m'a conféré le titre très honorifique et non officiel de « Photographe de

J'ai commencé à faire mes propres images en 2010 et n'ai cessé depuis, de passer par de multiples phases. J'essaie un peu tout pour me familiariser avec mon boîtier et trouver la sensibl photographique qui me convien le plus. J'ai fini par remporter ce concours au terme d'une belle compétition pleine d'adrénaline de rebondissements, ce qui m'a conféré le titre très honorifique non officiel de « Photographe de

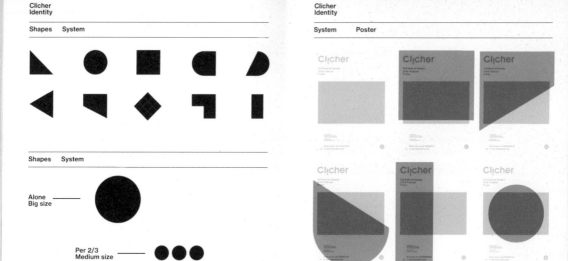

Shapes    System

Alone
Big size ———

Per 2/3 ———
Medium size

Infinite ———
Small size

Les formes peuvent être utiliser
séparemment ou ensemble.
Les tailles et couleurs des formes
peuvent varier autant que possible.

Les formes peuvent être utiliser
séparemment ou ensemble.
Les tailles et couleurs des formes
peuvent varier autant que possible.

signage for new office building
Monier based on its cubistic and
solid design.

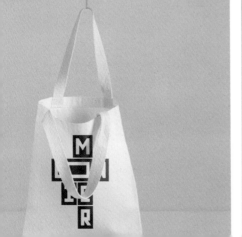

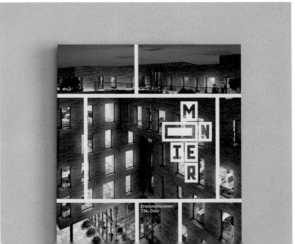

**07_Monier Logo, 2015.**
Design derived from Monier's three different window shapes that characterise the new office tower.

YME
Karl Johansgate 39
0157 Oslo, Norway
THE LINE
76 Greene Street, 3rd Floor
New York, NY 10012, US

M
FOUNDER

TOMWOOD
Prinsensgate 20

MONA@T

A/W COL. 2016

PA

**08_Tomwood Visual Identity, 2016.** Logotype and stationery for a Norwegian jewellery and fashion brand, and an application that generates patterns for use on textiles. Photos courtesy of Tomwood.

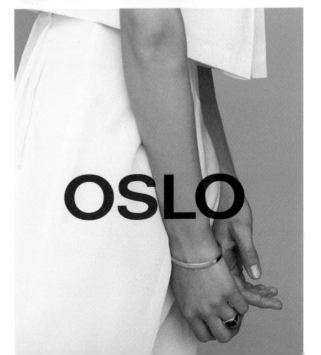

Branding themselves as "a new type of interference", ANTI has evolved from a design studio founded in 2008 into a full-service agency who wants to own all the areas of communication, including design, advertising, TV production, media and fashion. The team forges visual excellence and brand experience rooted in simplicity and good storytelling. Their union with Grandpeople and Non-Format reinforces their creative power and brand work with exceptional clout.

Oslo, Norway
Bergen, Norway
Hamar, Norway
Twin Cities, USA

• branding • graphics • digital design

# ANTI

**01_Rihanna x ANTI, 2016.** Self-initiated poster series made as gift for singer Rihanna during her ANTI World Tour Oslo Concert.

> "Architecture is not about the building itself, but how light and shadows work to define form."
>
> –
> ANTI

WE ARE
DARK
BUT NOT
THAT DARK

DARK

**02_Dark, 2016.** Brand concept aiming to create a vibrant, ever-changing profile that echoes Dark Arkitekter's mission to develop "living" cities.

**03_Dark (Web Design), 2016.**
Website interface playing with the concept of dark, light and shadows for Dark Arkitekter.

**04_DARK (Stationery), 2016.**
Stationery suite creates an extremely graphic and clean-cut profile that plays on Dark Arkitekter's name.

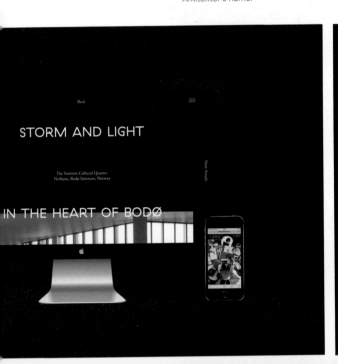

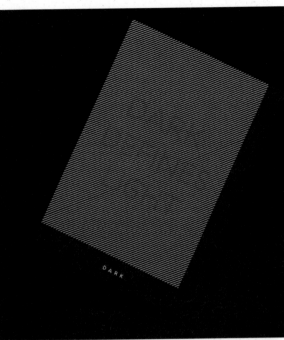

**05_Dublett, 2013-16.** Publication design for Dublett, a series of books that are partly an artist's work and partly produced by the same artist.

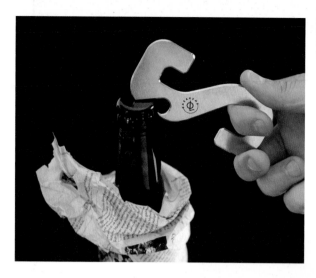

**06_Talasi, 2015.** Packaging design for Basarene ØL that incorporates local saying "Talas", meaning "speak soon", into a beer bottle concept.

homework

COPENHAGEN
/DENMARK

**What define(s) good design?**

Good design makes life better. We believe in simplifying messages in order for the essential to shine. We understand the importance of aspirational designs as a strategic business advantage for added commercial value — no matter how complex the project.

**What was your vision when you started your practice?**

Our visions are to build beautiful brands, challenge the way people feel and think by making design matter, contribute to a positive development by generating objects of desire, live a valuable life and do good design. We also wanted to collaborate with some of the most respected national and international brands within their fields and develop long-term relationships with clients.

**How would you describe your creative style?**

The signature aesthetic of Homework balances both timeless and contemporary design. We define how brands stay relevant and believe in simplifying the language so that the essential pops.

**What draw(s) you to stay in Denmark to work?**

The north is our home, where we live while working and focussing on both professional and personal efficiency. We have no problem working with international clients from our Danish base.

**What are your biggest influences? How do they work their way into your creations?**

We pride ourselves on being able to create a vast visual repertoire, driven by the combination of modern inspiration, research, our understanding of design history and retro references. Currently we are enamoured by sculptures and organic shapes, exploring the earthy tones, textures, tactility and relaxed simplicity we call "warm minimalism". In contrast we also throw ourselves into 60's and 70's retro referential design and art from Japan and worldwide, research into graphics, logos and illustrations.

**How do you ensure ideas/messages can be communicated effectively through your work?**

Each project has its own set of unique requirements but a constant one is to balance both the creative and the commercial viability. Collaborating with clients through a relationship based on mutual respect rids the project of unnecessary noise and strengthens the core ideas. The design should then enhance and support the underlying cause or message, not overshadow it.

**Can you name one thing that people normally would mistake and one thing people should know about "Nordic style"?**

A misconception about the Nordic style and minimalism is that if the visual language is minimalistic, the message is fundamentally easy or simple. The heritage of Nordic design has proved again and again that in minimalism no detail is trivial. This seemingly effortless style demands an immense sense of proportion and an eye for design and form. Sometimes the understated speaks volumes.

**Any upcoming projects?**

Homework has been blessed with amazing and inspiring clients over the years. Current projects in the making include work for Valentino Perfumes and Lancôme Beauty. Also on the horizon are the catalogue design for Republic of Fritz Hansen — home of iconic Danish furniture, among other brand identity projects.

**TEAM**

**Jack Dahl Sakurai**
Creative Director & Founder

**Stine Norup,**
**Regitze Frank**
Design & Account Managers

**Agnete Emilie Gjølby Melgaard**
Senior Art Director & Graphic
Designer

**Laura Brøchner-Mortensen,**
**Eleanor Bock Lund**
Junior Graphic Designers

Multidisciplinary design studio Forest specialises in graphic design, illustration and art direction. Founded in 2005 by Anna Katrin Karlsson and Johanne Halvorsen, who both studied visual communication at Oslo National Academy of the Arts, Forest works closely with clients, producing thoughtful visuals and graphics to fit brand profiles, editorials, album covers and the television screen. The duo leads a small and flexible team, always ready to embrace new challenges worldwide.

**01_Akershus Kunstsenter (Posters), 2016-.** Promotional materials for Akershus Art Centre's exhibitions, using primarily lines and colours to create a distinct and yet diverse graphic identity.

**02_Oslo Vegetarfestival, 2016-17.**
Posters and visual identity for the annual Vegetarian Festival in Oslo, Norway. Illustrations for the 2016 fruit-
themed editions were created jointly with Sofie Ensby Rostad.

**03_Make Me Some Music, 2015.** Collage and album cover design made as self-initiated project to explore creative possibilities without client restrictions and compromise.

Donau
Green is green
Marta
Canal Street
Son Da
Lona the Lion
Beginning of a conversation

Helsinki native Janine Rewell feels a strong connection with geometries. Stretching over categories and dimensions, her distinct illustration works are characterised by vector lines and vivid, colourful compositions charged with dreamy elements and a love for nature. Artistically trained at the University of Art and Design Helsinki and the Rhode Island School of Design, Rewell has been working independently since 2006 and is represented worldwide.

**Helsinki, Finland**

• identity • illustration
• editorial

# Janine Rewell

**01_NOOKS Dollhouse, 2015.** Seven interconnectable dollhouses with different visual themes, handmade and painted in Finland. Photos by Juho Huttunen.

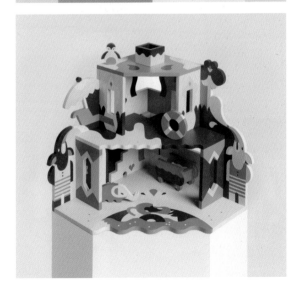

**02_NOOKS Dollhouse (Characters), 2015.** Characters designed to accompany the seven interconnectable dollhouses handmade and painted in Finland. Photos by Juho Huttunen.

**03_Lotte World Mall, 2016.**
Illustrations for the Seoul shopping mall's summer campaign, imagining a tropical jungle island rising from a cool summer sea. Production & display compositions by TIST Agency. Represented by Agent Pekka.

**04_LOTTE WORLD MALL, 2016.** Indoor installations presenting a blue paradise for the Seoul-based mall's summer campaign. Production & display compositions by TIST Agency. Represented by Agent Pekka.

**05_POLVELLA, 2016.** Childhood memories-inspired illustrations and wooden art pieces created for Rewell's exhibitions in China, organised by Shenzhen Illustration Association, and in Finland.

**06_ISETAN FIKA, 2016.** Skiing-themed illustration
for Scandinavian deli Fika's cookie packaging sold by
Japanese department store ISETAN.

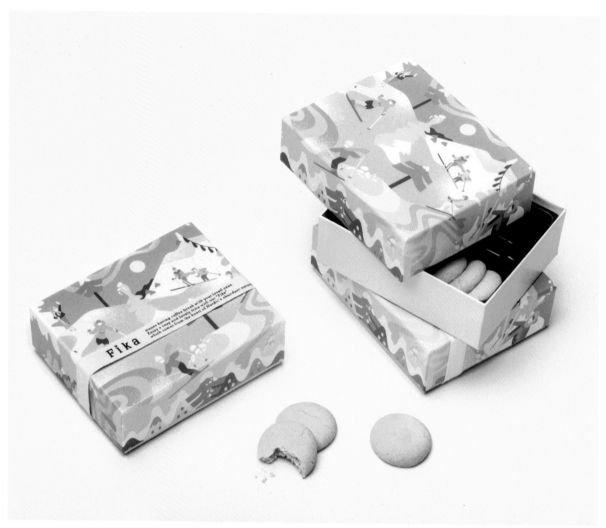

**07_ISETAN FIKA, 2015.** Illustration for Scandinavian deli Fika's festive cookie packaging sold by Japanese department store ISETAN.

Establishing himself under the name "Sig Vicious", Siggeir Magnús Hafsteinsson identifies himself partly as a graphic designer, and partly a radical neo-avant-garde visual artist. A rebel at heart, the self-taught artist constantly seeks to challenge creative boundaries and build imagery that highlight the contrasts of textures, colours and forms. Iceland's striking landscapes, rural/urban street photography, abstract music artwork and collage prints are some of his favourite subjects to explore.

**Reykjavík, Iceland**

• graphics • photography

# Siggeir Magnús Hafsteinsson

**01_Lavastract (Part 1), 2015-17.** Collage images blending Icelandic nature, photography and graphics. On this page: Silicone. On facing page, anti-clockwise from upper left: Sinistarr, Electrocution, Lavatecture, Rok.

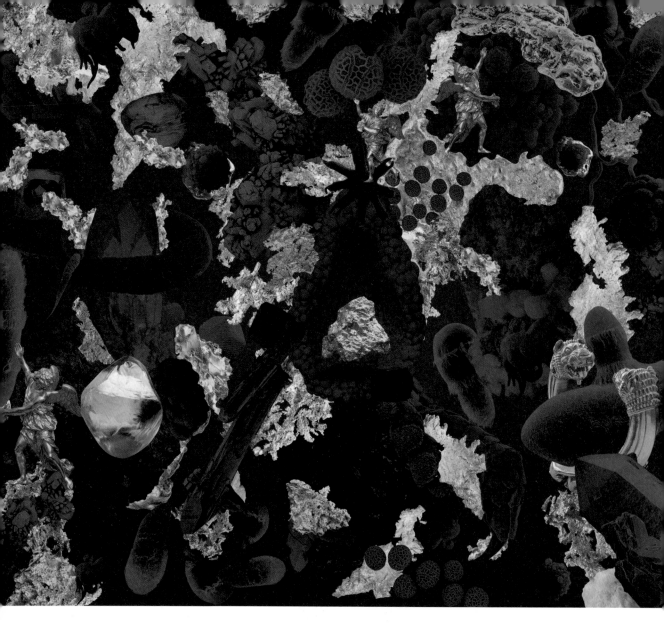

**02_Lavastract (Part 2), 2015-17.** Collage images blending Icelandic nature, photography and graphics. Above: Dark Gold Ultra. Bottom, left to right: Sulphur, Green Gorge.

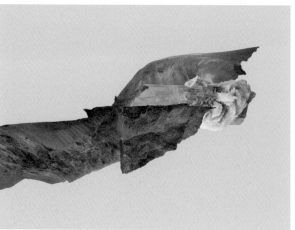

**03_Lavastract: Stairway To Heaven, 2015-17.**
Collage image made from pictures of Icelandic nature.

SIGGEIR MAGNÚS HAFSTEINSSON —— 302/303

HZN064

**AMOSS**
BUMBACLART / DILATE

SIG VICIOUS

**04_Horizons Music (Amoss), 2013.** Vinyl sleeve and poster design for drum and bass band Amoss, part of ongoing art direction project for label Horizons Music.

**05_Horizons Music (Mikal & Serum).**
Vinyl sleeves and posters designed for
bands Mikal (top) and Serum (bottom),
part of ongoing art direction project
for label Horizons Music.

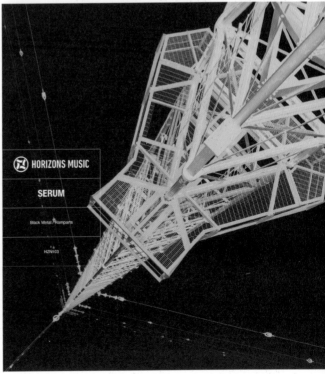

**"Ever since the first aluminium factory opened in Straumsvík in 1969, the industry has had a steady growth here largely supported by low-cost electricity. Álvera represents the way I see the industry here in Iceland."**

–

SIGGEIR MAGNÚS HAFSTEINSSON

**06_Alvera, 2016.** Self-initiated project, using photography to connect the aluminium industry with Iceland, a subject of ongoing national debate.

# INDEX

## ACKNOWLEDGEMENTS

We would like to thank all the designers and companies who
have involved in the production of this book. This project
would not have been accomplished without their significant
contribution to the compilation of this book.
We would also like to express our gratitude to all the producers
for their invaluable opinions and assistance throughout this
entire project. The successful completion also owes a great
deal to many professionals in the creative industry who have
given us precious insights and comments. And to the many
others whose names are not credited but have made specific
input in this book, we thank you for your continuous support
the whole time.

## FUTURE EDITIONS

If you wish to participate in viction:ary's future projects and
publications, please send your website or portfolio to
submit@victionary.com